W0037022

HALLE · ZEIT · WACH · 1842

Antonio L. Furtado Erich J. Neuhold

Formal Techniques for Data Base Design

With 35 Figures

Springer-Verlag
Berlin Heidelberg New York Tokyo

Prof. Dr. Antonio L. Furtado
Pontificia Universidade Católica do Rio de Janeiro
Rio de Janeiro/Brasilien

Prof. Dr. Erich J. Neuhold
Institut für
Angewandte Informatik und Systemanalyse
Technische Universität Wien
Paniglgasse 16, A-1040 Wien

In Collaboration with:

M.A. Casanova, IBM do Brasil
P.A.S. Veloso, Pontificia Universidade Católica do Rio de Janeiro

ISBN-13: 978-3-642-70594-6 e-ISBN-13: 978-3-642-70592-2
DOI: 10.1007/978-3-642-70592-2

Library of Congress Cataloging in Publication Data. Furtado, Antonio Luz. Formal techniques for data base design. Bibliography: p. Includes index. 1. Data base management. 2. System design. I. Neuhold, Erich J. II. Title. QA76.9.D3N47 1986 001.64 85-12633
ISBN-13: 978-3-642-70594-6

Softcover reprint of the hardcover 1st edition 1986

Typsetting, printing and bookbinding: Graphischer Betrieb Konrad Triltsch, Würzburg
2145/3140-543210

Preface

We report here the results obtained thus far along two distinct but complementary and converging lines of research work. The theme is conceptual data base design (specification), and the work has been going on for a number of years, mainly at the University of Stuttgart, in the Federal Republic of Germany, and at the Pontificia Universidade Católica do Rio de Janeiro, in Brasil.

We are glad to acknowledge the collaboration of several colleagues and students, particularly H. Biller, J. M. V. de Castilho, A. Horndasch, C. S. dos Santos, R. Studer, U. Schiel, and I. Walter. Two other co-workers deservey special recognition, since they have shared in writing the report which originated part A of this book – M. A. Casanova and P. A. S. Veloso.

The book is intended as a text for graduate courses on information systems and on data bases. The subject is treated formally, since we do believe that formality leads to precision, a quality that one misses in the still prevailing ad-hoc techniques. The theoretical background is covered, although in a condensed fashion, referring the reader to the appropriate literature for more details.

November 1985

A.L. Furtado
E.J. Neuhold

Table of Contents

1 General Introduction – Two Approaches to Formal Data Base Design . 1

Part A – Application-Oriented Approach 5

2 Introduction to Part A 7

3 An Informal Outline 9

3.1 Information Level 9
3.2 Functions Level 10
3.3 Representation Level 12
3.4 Placing the Formalisms 13

4 The Information Level – The Use of Logical Formalisms 15

4.1 Logical Formalisms 15
4.2 An Example 17

5 The Functions Level – The Use of Algebraic Formalisms 19

5.1 Algebraic Formalisms 19
5.2 Obtaining a Functions Level Specification – An Example 20
5.3 First to Second Level Refinements 23
5.4 Proof of Correctness of the Refinement – An Example 26

6 The Representation Level –
The Use of a Programming Language Formalism 29

6.1 Programming Language Formalism 29
6.1.1 Syntax – The Use of a Grammatical Formalism. 29
6.1.2 Semantics – The Use of a Denotational Formalism 34
6.2 Obtaining a Representation Level Specification – An Example . . . 37
6.3 Second to Third Level Refinements. 38
6.4 Proof of Correctness of the Refinement – An Example 40

Part B – Semantic Data Models 45

7 Introduction to Part B 47

8 The Logical Database Model 49

8.1 The Semantic Framework 51
8.1.1 Reality and the Real World States 52
8.1.2 The Natural Language State Description 53

8.1.3 The Abstract Model and the Standard Interpretation . . . 53
8.1.4 The Logical State Description and the Interpretation I_{DB} . . 54
8.1.5 Conventional Data Bases – The Syntactical View 57
8.2 The Logical Data Definition Language 58
8.2.1 Type Declarations 59
8.2.2 The <Type Definition> Clause of a Type Declaration . . . 60
8.2.3 The <Characteristics> Clause of a Type Declaration 62
8.2.4 The <Identification> Clause of a Type Declaration 63
8.2.5 Relation Declarations 65
8.2.6 The <Domain Definitions> Clause of Relation Declarations. 65
8.2.7 The <Consistency Constraints> Clause of Relation Declarations 65
8.3 The Logical Data Language LDL 67

9 The Entity-Relationship Model 71

9.1 The Entity-Relationship-Value Concept 72
9.1.1 Level 1: Entities, Relationships, Values. 72
9.1.2 Level 2: Entity-Relationship Diagram 75
9.1.3 Level 3: Entity Relations, Relationship Relations and Relation Tables 75
9.2 Data Types and the Entity-Relationship Model 78
9.2.1 Generalization/Specialization 79
9.2.2 Aggregation 81
9.2.3 Grouping 81
9.3 Existence and Identification Constraints in the Extended ER-Model 83
9.3.1 Constraints Related to Generalization/Specialization 83
9.3.2 Constraints Related to Aggregation 84
9.3.3 Constraints Related to Grouping 85
9.4 An Example Using the Extended ER-Model 85

10 The Temporal Hierarchic Model 87

10.1 The Basic Concepts of THM 87
10.2 The Notions of Time in THM 89
10.3 The Operational Facilities of the Temporal Hierarchic Model . . 93
10.3.1 The Basic State Manipulation Actions 95
10.3.2 Complex State Manipulation Actions 99

11 Conclusion 105

12 References. 107

13 Subject Index 113

1 General Introduction – Two Approaches to Formal Data Base Design

The purpose of this book is to discuss formal techniques for designing the data base component of information systems. We shall call each particular instance of this component a *data base application*. Moreover, since the design will be restricted to the conceptual aspects, stopping short of physical computer implementation, we shall use the terms design and *specification* interchangeably.

As the importance of data base technology was recognized, as an effective way to keep and manipulate large repositories of information, there was a proliferation of *Data Base Management Systems* (*DBMSs*), i.e. software products providing this function. To try to impose some discipline on this proliferation, there were attempts at standardization, which succeeded only partially. Instead of a single standard, different classes of DBMSs were identified.

The fundamental subject of *data models* emerged as a consequence of *abstracting* the essential aspects of these classes of DBMSs. More specifically, each data model is built around some *abstract data structure*. On the data structure a number of operations are defined and certain inherent integrity constraints are declared, ruling out some instances of the data structure as illegal. The three "major" data models and their respective underlying data structures are:

- hierarchical model – trees
- network model – graphs
- relational model – tables

The above characterization of data models corresponds to the notion of *abstract data types*. Well-known examples of abstract data types, from the area of programming languages, are stacks, arrays, lists, etc. Instances of the type stack can be manipulated by operations such as top, push, pop, which are constrained by a last-in-first-out discipline limiting access to the stack component located at its "top".

Arrays and lists have their own operations and inherent constraints, and it is interesting to note that their instances are somehow more general (less constrained) than stacks: in both types the respective operations allow access to any component, including therefore the top one. As a consequence, if our programming language supports, say, arrays as a built-in data type, we can *represent* the data type stack by the data type array. To make this representation safe, we must exclude the possibility to access any component of a stack instance (internally represented by an array instance) that is not the top component. This is usually done by:

- defining each stack operation (top, push, pop) in terms of "procedures" consisting of appropriate array operations;
- allowing only these procedures to be used, forbidding therefore that the programmer invoke directly the primitive array operations.

This strategy is known as *encapsulation* and is enforced either through constructs of the programming language (variously called clusters, modules, etc.) or by the programmer's self-discipline, when no such constructs are available.

Returning to our subject, since we regard data models as abstract data types we can proceed along the same line of reasoning to identify particular data base applications also as abstract data types. Being more general than the applications, data models should be able to represent them. Thus, we are led to talk of representing an academic data base, say, by the relational or by the network data model, in exactly the same sense that we speak of the representation of stacks by arrays or by lists.

If we have a DBMS belonging to the class of a given data model, then, after representing our data base application by the data model, we are in a position to achieve a concrete computer implementation through the detailed coding of this (still abstract) representation, using the commands of the DBMS. We should stress this distinction between

- the abstract representation, using the data model;
- the concrete implementation, on a DBMS of the class of the data model.

The former step belongs to the specification phase, which rationality imposes as a necessary prerequisite to implementation. Yet, there are some disadvantages in limiting the specification phase to abstract representations on top of a data model, as we shall argue in the sequel.

Data models have been criticized for their lack of *semantics*, that is, for their inability to capture the *meaning* of information and its *behavior* with regard to activities pertaining to the application. In short, data models offer abstractions of computer phenomena involving files and computer processing, rather than abstractions of real world phenomena. The consequence is that the distance between the application, as perceived by its human agents, and a data model, leading to a computer implementation, is too wide. The data model does not offer adequate help towards an understanding of the application; in fact data models require design decisions that cannot be taken in view of purely "abstract" criteria, but demand instead that the characteristics of the application be well-understood.

Figure 1.1 depicts this "semantic gap" problem. It will become clear in the sequel that the main difference between the two alternative approaches, taken in parts A and B of this book, is how to fill up the gap.

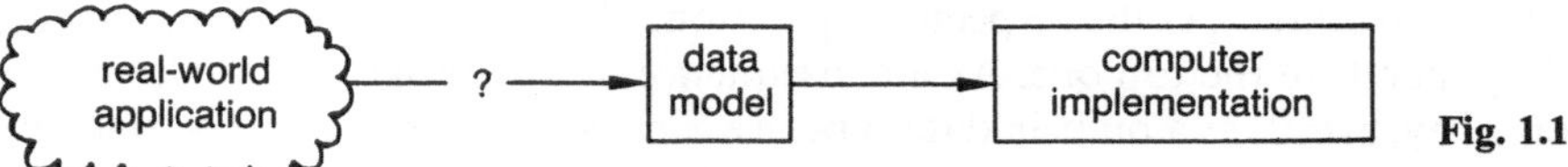

Fig. 1.1

How can we specify an application without a data model? This is the same as specifying any (simpler) data type without referring to how we shall eventually represent it. Always resorting to the simple example of stacks, in an array representation we might write, as part of an operation to push v into stack A (in a PASCAL-like language):

t := t + 1;
A [t] := v

and then a top function to access stack A would have:

top := A [t]

this being a consequence of the last-in-first-out requirement for stacks. But this requirement can be formally stated, for example by the equation:

top (push (v, A)) = v

Notice also that the equation does not mention (and is therefore independent of) the representation that we use for stacks, be it array or list representation. The equation proceeds by showing how top and push interact. In data base terminology, we would say that it shows how the *query operation* (top) is affected by the *update operation* (push).

The argument would stop here in the case of simple data types like stacks, where all the semantic considerations are those implicit in the definition of its operations. For data base applications, however, the *information* itself must be characterized before the *functions* (operations) that utilize it.

Accordingly, PART A of the book, which adopts an *application-oriented approach*, distinguishes three levels of specification:

- the informations level;
- the functions level;
- the representation level.

The first two levels are independent of the choice of data model, and are sufficient if no future computer implementation is envisioned. Data models appear only at the third level.

Many formalisms have been proposed in the literature for the specification of data bases, and we might choose a single one for all levels. Although this may be possible, we took the attitude that formalisms should not be forced beyond their original intended scope. Accordingly, we adopted an eclectic approach, thus facing the complex task of going from one level to the next passing through different formalisms.

A radically different approach to bridge the gap between real-world applications and data models is taken in PART B. This approach involves *semantic data models*, known also as information models [ISO]. In semantic data models the modelling features are oriented towards real-world phenomena. Research in the area of artificial intelligence, especially on *knowledge bases*, vitally contributes to this line of work.

Three models of increasing expressive power are presented:

In the *Logic Data Model* atomic (unstructured) objects are used as abstractions of real world entities. The properties of these real world entities are then modelled by object classification (typing) on one side and relationships between objects (classes) on the other. Classes may be overlapping, e.g. a person may be both an employee and a shareholder of a company, and usually contain objects that share at least one common property beyond the fact of being a member of the class.

In the *Entity Relationship Model*, atomic objects may be combined into more complex objects which themselves recursively form even more complex objects. Complex objects like atomic objects represent some unit of discourse in the real world, e.g. a department, a company, and have properties which are not just derivations of properties of their components, e.g. a department manager, a company name.

In the *Temporal Hierarchic Model* the abstract data type principles are utilized to provide the system and application operations which can be used to manipulate the various objects, object classes and relationships in the model. In addition they are used to restrict the manipulation of objects to precisely those provided operations, thus enabling the enforcement of the various constraints on the data base that restrict the syntactically possible states to precisely those that are meaningful when considered with respect to the real world. Examples of such operations are create-new-object, which is a very basic operation creating a not further specified new entity in the data base. This entity then receives meaning by operations like make-person (object-id) or hire-person (person-id), etc. To represent the real world, time considerations cannot be excluded, e.g. date-of-hire, duration-of-employment, former-employee, and the Temporal Hierarchic Model provides for the necessary basic mechanisms that allow such specifications.

Part A

Application-Oriented Approach

2 Introduction to Part A

Different groups of researchers have been using different formalisms in connection with data bases. Here we shall consider the use of formalisms with the following primary purpose:

To specify data base applications subjected to intergrity constraints.

Initially, we would like to concentrate on the characteristics of the data base application being specified, with no concern for its eventual computer implementation. Such concern would be brought to the foreground after those characteristics are well understood. To guide the phase of implementation-oriented specification, the auxiliary purpose below must also be served:

To specify features of data models, to be used for adapting data base applications to computing environments.

What aspects should be covered in this double-purpose specification process? A data base application is first of all a repository of time-varying *information*. Secondly, there must be *functions* whereby the information will be used, i.e. interrogated or changed. Thirdly, as we move towards an implementation, we must provide a *representation* for the data base according to some chosen data model, which involves expressing how the information will be structured and the functions programmed. In turn, the data model specification has *syntactical* and *semantical* aspects.

Although data base theory has been largely influenced by concepts derived from *first-order logic*, either in pure form or adapted to the particular needs of data base research, there have been many attempts to use *algebra*, high-level *programming language constructs*, *grammars* and *denotational semantics* to capture data base concepts. One might claim that each formalism is powerful enough to cover many (or perhaps all) aspects listed. However it seems more reasonable to conjecture that a single formalism will probably not be equally convenient for all aspects. This position, which we also take, has led to the notion of *complementarity*.

The major contribution of this research lies in selecting the correct variation of each formalism for each level of specification, in the style of organizing the formalisms together into a coherent *conceptual design framework* and in the formal notion of refinement binding the different levels. Thus, contrarily to most published literature, we neither limit ourselves to just one formalism at just one level nor force the use of the same formalism at different levels, which often creates distortions. Finally, although not intended to be a survey of the area, this text may serve as a guide to different approaches to data base theory.

We divide the design process into three levels of specification. Before embarking on their rigorous characterization, we explore them informally in Chap. 3, where the overly simplified example to be used as illustration is also introduced. In the next paragraphs we briefly say what are these levels of specification, as we indicate how the rest of part A is organized.

The first level, the *information level*, characterizes the data base by its information contents independently of how the information will be used or represented. It gives a high-level description of the set of consistent data base states and the set of state transitions and typically involves a language to talk about the data base and a set of static constraints indicating which states are considered consistent, and a set of transition constraints indicating in turn which transitions are acceptable. We will adopt an extension of first-order languages, as described in Chap. 4.

At the second level, the *functions level*, we add to the characterization of a data base a repertoire of functions, establishing how we intend to use the information. These functions indicate how the data base will be queried or updated and depend on the applications the designer anticipates for the data base. We will use an algebraic formalism related to abstract data types, which is described in Chap. 5.

The third and final level, the *representation level*, specifies the data base with the help of a data model. A representation of the data base in terms of the data structures supported by the data model must be found and the functions defined at the second level must be mapped into procedures using a Data Manipulation Language (DML) associated with the model. The third level therefore brings us close to the implementation of the data base application on top of a Data Base Management System (DBMS). A programming language, described in Chap. 6, will be used to specify the data base at the third level. The syntax of the language is given by a grammatical formalism, W-grammars, and its semantics is described using a denotational formalism.

Each level of specification must be a *refinement* of the previous one, in the sense that the second-level update functions must preserve the first-level static and transition constraints, and the third-level procedures defining second-level functions must satisfy the second-level equations. This is further discussed in Sect. 5.3 and 6.3.

3 An Informal Outline

3.1 Information Level

At the first level, we consider that data bases will contain instances of *facts*, defined as positive assertions about the application area. Usually, negative facts are not stored (such as what courses are *not* taken by a student). A *state* is the collection of facts that are true at a given instant of time; therefore, a state denotes the entire contents of the data base at that instant. *Static constraints* are restrictions defined on states. A *valid state* is one that conforms to all specified static constraints.

A *transition* is a state transformation. A transition can be denoted by a pair of states. Again we may want to impose restrictions on transitions. Thus a *valid transition*, besides being required to involve only valid states, must conform to the declared *transition constraints*.

We now begin to present the simple academic data base example to be used throughout the discussion. Using the terminology of the first level, we have:

Facts:	– courses are offered – students take courses		
Static Constraint:	students can only be taking currently offered courses		
Example of a Valid State:	c1 is offered c2 is offered John takes c1		
Transition Constraint:	the number of courses taken by a student cannot drop to zero (during the academic term)		
Example of a Valid Transition:	c1 is offered c2 is offered John takes c1	⟶	c1 is offered c2 is offered John takes c2

Certain points not explicit in our unrealistically simple example must now be stressed. The first point is *time*, implicitly involved in the transition constraint, which applies only during the current academic term. Time appears in many ways: simply as a criterion to order states, as a duration, as a date, etc. Next we observe that the size and complexity of realistic data bases make their direct specification in one piece an impracticable task. *Modularization* is in order. Also, we must have ways to verify properties of specifications, such as consistency, non-redundancy, etc., both within and across the various modules.

In an "intelligent" data base, one should be able to *infer* certain facts, which then would not have to be stored. For example, if we are confident that the current state of our academic data base is valid and that John takes c1, we could deduce that c1 is offered, taking our static constraint as a *general law*. Inference becomes more complex when states are allowed to include alternative facts such as John takes c1 *or* c2, or facts with indeterminate values, such as John takes some course, whose name is presently unknown (an *undefined value*).

3.2 Functions Level

We now turn to the second level, where functions are introduced. To each fact there corresponds a *query function* to check whether or not the fact holds; *update functions* provide the means to effect transitions, taking states into states. To indicate how a new state is obtained from the current one, we shall *assert* the facts that become true and *deny* those that cease to be true. Because of the integrity constraints, the application of certain functions becomes dependent on *pre-conditions.*

The choice of the set of functions is dictated by the needs of the specific data base application that one can anticipate. In our example the query functions will be:

is course being offered?
is student taking course?

with the obvious meaning. The update functions will be:

initiate academic term:	– the data base is "empty" (all facts false)
offer course:	– assert that the course is offered
cancel course:	– if no student takes the course then deny that the course is offered
enroll student in course:	– if the course is offered then assert that the student takes the course
transfer student from course1 to course2:	– if the student takes course1 and does not take course2 and course2 is offered then deny that the student takes course1 and assert that he takes course2

Note that here no formal meaning is attached to words like "assert", "deny", "if... then"; they are used only to favor more concise and structured natural language descriptions.

When we associate application-oriented functions with actions happening in the real world, we are assuming that reality is changed only when the corresponding functions succeed in updating the data base in the intended way. In other words, the segment of interest of the real world is indistinguishable from the data base. It becomes physically impossible to perform an action that violates some policy of the organization, expressed as a constraint. Also, we can automate certain actions, achieving the so-called *active systems*, where actions can be triggered by the occurrence of *events* (possibly involving stored facts, time, etc.).

There may be more than one way to design functions that effectively preserve the declared constraints, which implies that more than one second level specification would be compatible with (and therefore not entirely determined by) the first level specification. Part of this freedom of choice comes from the existence of different ways to combine pre-conditions and effects and also to decide between actions initiated by users and triggered actions. To discuss these possibilities we shall employ the example below.

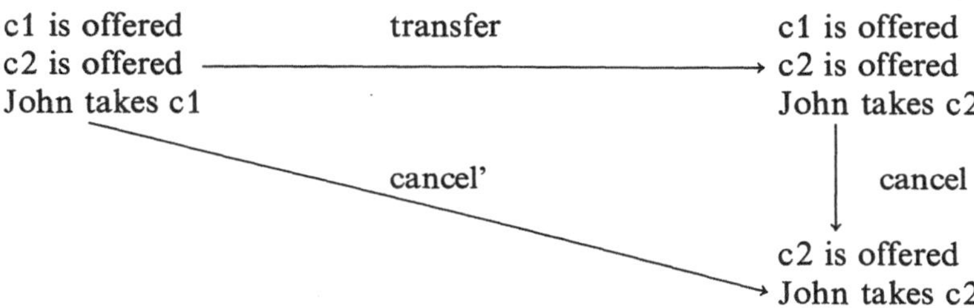

With the present definition of the functions we could not execute cancel c1 at the state where John takes this course, whereas the use of cancel is legal at the state reached by transferring John to c2. This suggests that, in order to make cancel applicable at the first state shown, we might redefine cancel (see cancel' above) by expanding its effects, thereby being able to weaken its pre-conditions.

Besides redefining a function we may want to create additional ones. For instance, we might add an operation allowing a student to drop a course, if it is not the only one that he is currently taking. Finally, if we had both drop and transfer functions, we could achieve the modified effect of cancel' indicated above without redefining the function: we would merely add a trigger causing either drop or transfer to be invoked for each student taking c1.

The order of execution of operations, on the other hand, is not entirely free because of the interplay of pre-conditions and effects. In our example, enroll John in c1 can only be executed after offer c1 has been executed. Functions whose effects are necessary to fulfill pre-conditions of other functions entail *serial execution*. On the contrary, offer c1 and offer c2, for instance, can be executed *in parallel*.

Also from the study of the interplay of pre-conditions and effects, one can conclude that different sequences of functions can accomplish the same net result. Calling a *trace* any sequence of update functions starting at the initial empty state, the two traces:

offer c1 . offer c2 . enroll John in c1 . transfer John from c1 to c2 . cancel c1

and

offer c2 . enroll John in c2

lead to the same state and are in this sense *equivalent*. Traces clearly provide an alternative way to denote the states that they generate.

3.3 Representation Level

To run a data base application on a machine we must adapt the data base application to the machine environment. Such environments involve file structures and facilities to declare, access and manipulate them, usually constituting a *Data Base Management System* (*DBMS*).

This adaptation can be specified independently from actual machine details if we employ the *abstract structure* provided by some *data model*. The current data models offer trees, graphs, tables, etc. as abstract structures. To each data model there corresponds a family of DBMSs.

Using the *relational model*, we could represent the information in our academic data base by way of two tables, OFFERED and TAKES, as shown below:

OFFERED

C#
c1
c2
..

TAKES

S#	C#
John	c1
...	..
...	..

Executing a query function will now correspond to inspecting tuples of the appropriate tables whereas, for an update function, certain tuples will be inserted, deleted or modified. For instance, transferring John from c1 to c2 involves (after an inspection that would show the presence of tuple (c1) in OFFERED, the absence of (John, c2) from TAKES and the presence of (John, c1) in TAKES) the deletion of (John, c1) from and the insertion of (John, c2) in TAKES.

One would expect a DBMS to handle constraints in at least one of the following ways:

a) The constraint may be *implicit* in the data model. An example is that relational tables, by definition, do not admit duplicate tuples.
b) The constraint may be *declared*. For example, we may declare that certain columns of a table constitute a *key*, in which case no two tuples with the same values in such columns are permitted.
c) The constraint may be enforced *procedurally*. This can be accomplished, among other ways, by restricting tuple-update operations to be invoked only from within procedures corresponding to the previously defined update functions. An example is the description above of how transfer would be executed on the OFFERED and TAKES tables.

Since strategy a) is not enough and most DBMSs are weak in terms of features to enable strategy b), strategy c), known as *encapsulation*, becomes an important option and is assumed here. A characteristic of encapsulation is that it does not prevent that the execution of tuple-update operations violate constraints; however this occurs only at *intermediate states*. For example, when transferring John from c1 to c2, as we first delete (John, c1) from TAKES the transition constraint is violated, but the violation is immediately corrected by the ensuing insertion of (John, c2).

Similarly to the relationship between levels one and two, there can be more than one third level specification compatible with a second level one, in the sense that all functions are correctly realized. Here the freedom results from the possibility of choosing among different data models and also from the various ways whereby a data base application can be structured within the same data model.

3.4 Placing the Formalisms

We have investigated, in some detail, the nature of what we want to specify formally. In the introduction, five formalisms were mentioned. We now propose that each formalism be used essentially for the purpose that originally motivated its conception:

- with respect to data base applications
  - for the information level – logical formalism
  - for the functions level – algebraic formalism
  - for the representation level – programming language formalism

The basic formalism is logic. For a long time, first-order logic has been regarded as a paradigm of formalization.

The first level of specification characterizes data bases by their information contents, independently of how the information will be used and also independently of representation. We did not see any need to depart from logic at this level, where types of facts will quite naturally correspond to *predicate symbols* and integrity constraints to *axioms*. Yet, we note that considerations, such as the presence of components of different types and transition constraints, may prescribe the use of many-sorted first-order logic and temporal logic, rather than strict first-order logic.

At the second level, we add to the characterization of a data base a repertoire of functions, establishing how we intend to use the information. Representation considerations are still absent. Algebraic formalisms have been conceived precisely to specify objects by the collection of functions defined on them. Functions will be defined via *conditional equations* expressing their input/output properties.

At the third level we introduce representation, following a data model, and thus pave the way to an eventual computer implementation. When indicating what kinds of information the data base will contain (at the first level) no thought is given to how it could be structured for efficient access. Similarly, the functions defined (at the second level) take entire data base states both as domain and range, whereas, if the information were organized, inspections and changes could be circumscribed to small parts of the data base. The formalisms that more directly express computing phenomena are programming languages. With the commands of a programming language, functions can be programmed as *procedures*, acting on *data structures* containing the information. (see also [We2], page 158, for three-level specifications).

A programming language to be employed for formal specification must, of course, be a very high-level and theoretically sound language, which excludes most languages coming with the currently available DBMSs. Moreover, it must itself be formally specified, and thus we have:

- with respect to the language associated with the data model
  - for the syntactical aspects – grammatical formalism
  - for the semantical aspects – denotational formalism

Grammatical formalisms have indeed been created for specifying syntax. They describe it by way of *production rules*. Certain "context-sensitive" syntactical aspects have been misleadingly labelled as belonging to semantics, simply because of the inability of formalisms, such as BNF, to cope with them. Here, we shall use two-level grammars, which have enough power, for instance, to exclude syntactically commands that manipulate undeclared data structures.

Denotational formalisms purport to explain in mathematical terms the semantics of computer-oriented constructs. They sometimes also cover "abstract syntax", resorting to BNF productions. Since a fully comprehensive treatment of syntax can be provided as indicated in the previous paragraph, we can concentrate on the semantical aspects, to be described mainly by *semantic equations*.

We should pass from one level to the next in a *constructive* manner, and should also be able to *verify*, afterwards, that we have done so in a correct way, i.e., among other requirements:

a) that the second-level functions *preserve* the first-level integrity constraints;
b) that the third-level procedures *realize* the second-level functions.

The second requirement implies that a formal specification of the language used at the third level should be available beforehand.

4 The Information Level – The Use of Logical Formalisms

4.1 Logical Formalisms

In this section we briefly indicate how a data base can be specified, at the information level, using a logical formalism. We assume familiarity with first-order logic at the level, say, of [En], so that the presentation of the formalism will be very terse.

To set up basic terminology and notation, we recall that the alphabet of a *first-order language* consists of: (1) a set of logical symbols, which are the variables, the usual connectives and quantifiers, the equality symbol (if necessary), and parenthesis; (2) a set of non-logical symbols, which are a set of constant symbols and, for each positive integer n, a set of n-ary predicate symbols and a set of n-ary function symbols. Terms are built from variables, constants and function symbols using the familiar formation rules. Well-formed formulas (wffs) are constructed out of terms, predicate symbols (including equality) and connectives and quantifiers, again using the familiar formation rules. A literal is either an atomic wff or a negated atomic wff. A ground term is a term with no variables and, likewise, a ground wff is a wff with no variables.

A *structure* I for a first-order language L consists of a nonempty set D, the domain of I, and assigns to each constant c of L an element of D, to each n-ary function symbol f of L an n-ary function I(f) over D, and to each n-ary predicate symbol p of L an n-ary relation over D. A *valuation* of L for I is a function v assigning to each variable of L an element of D. We use $\models$ I P[v] to indicate that I satisfies P with v, and use $\models$ I P to indicate that I satisfies P with any valuation v of L for I [En]. In the last case, we say that P is *valid* in I. A *model* of a set W of wffs of L is a structure I of L such that all wffs in W are valid in I. We say that W *logically implies* a wff w iff w is valid in any model of W.

The *first-order predicate calculus* defined on a first-order language consists of a set of axiom schemes, the *logical axioms*, and two inference rules: modus ponens and generalization.

A *first-order axiomatic theory* is a pair T = (L, A), where L is a first-order language and A is a set of wffs of L, called the *non-logical* or *proper axioms* of the theory. A model of the theory is an interpretation of L in which all axioms are valid.

To conclude this brief refresher about first-order languages, we say that the language is *many-sorted* when each variable and constant is assigned to a sort, each n-ary predicate symbol p is associated with an n-tuple of sorts $\langle T1, \ldots, Tn \rangle$ (Ti is the sort of the i-th argument of p), and each n-ary function symbol is associated with an (n + 1)-tuple of sorts $\langle T1, \ldots, Tn+1 \rangle$ (Ti indicates the sort of the i-th argument, $0 < i < n+1$, and $Tn+1$, called the target sort, indicates the sort of the result). Moreover, the formation rules of terms and wffs are changed so that sorts are respected (for the details see [En]).

At the information level, a data base can in principle be adequately represented as a first-order theory T1 = (L1, A1), where L1 is a first-order language used to talk about the data base and A1 is a set of non-logical axioms essentially defining the set of consistent data base states.

A very rich vein of research during the past years has centered around special classes of first-order sentences that capture important facts about data bases and yet have special properties not shared by the full version of first-order logic. The various classes of data dependencies offer the best example.

In another direction, variations of first-order logic have been used to express data base concepts that cannot be readily expressed by ordinary first-order languages. Aggregation operations, such as SUM and AVERAGE that map relations into scalar objects, is one example. They require a special treatment to avoid talking about higher-order functions of higher-order logics [CB].

Another example is precisely the notion of transition constraints that impose restrictions on data base state transitions and not just on data base states. Most of the research, with a few notable exceptions, ignored this type of constraints, although they are equally important and interesting. We now explain a possible extension of first-order languages to cover aspects related to transitions. The extension we describe is perhaps the simplest one and depends on the introduction of two *modal operators*. Other sets of modal operators can be adapted to enhance the expressive power of the language. A different approach could also be taken by selecting a many-sorted first-order language with a special sort interpreted as time (see [CF, CCF, MWJ, BADW] for extensive discussions).

Given a (many-sorted) first-order language L, its *temporal extension*, LT, is defined as follows. The symbols of LT are those of L, plus one *modal operator*, the possibility operator denoted by '$\Diamond$'. The modal operator $\Box$ of necessity is the dual of $\Diamond$ in that it can be introduced by definition as $\Box P \equiv \sim \Diamond \sim P$. The terms of LT are those of L and the set of wffs of L is defined using the familiar formation rules, plus one new rule:

if P is a wff of L or LT, then $\Diamond P$ is also a wff of LT

The semantics of LT is defined as follows. A *universe* U for LT is a pair (S, R), where S is a set of structures of L, all with the same domain D (this restriction can be relaxed, but it simplifies the treatment of quantifiers), and R is a binary relation over S, called the *accessibility relation*. Given a wff P of LT, a structure I in S and a valuation v over the common domain D, we define the notion that *I satisfies P with v in U* (denoted $\models$ UI P[v]) using rules identical to those of first-order languages, plus one additional rule:

$\models$ UI ($\Diamond$ P)[v] iff there is J in S such that R(I, J) and $\models$ UJ P[v]

A wff of LT without any modal operator is called a *static wff*. A fully temporal wff is conveniently viewed as consisting of static subformulas to which modal operators have been applied.

The notions of model, logical implication and theory are as for first-order languages.

Thus, to account for transition constraints, a data base is specified at the information level by defining a theory $T1 = (L1, A1)$, where $L1$ is a temporal extension of a (many-sorted) first-order language L and $A1$ is a set of axioms. The non-logical symbols of $L1$ describe the data base data structures and all ordinary symbols, such as "less than", used to express facts about the data base. Data base structures are represented by special predicate symbols, called *db-predicate symbols*. The axioms in $A1$ define static constraints, if they do not involve modal operators (i.e. are static wffs), or transition constraints, otherwise. The semantics of the data base is fixed by selecting a universe $U = (S, R)$ for $L1$. The structures in S play the role of data base states and the relation R over S is interpreted as indicating that, if (I, J) is in R, then J is a future state with respect to I. A structure I in S corresponds to a consistent state iff it is a model of $T1$.

We note that the semantics of a data base, as explained above, is only loosely fixed by the theory $T1$, especially the relation R. This situation is modified when the functions level (i.e., algebraic) specification of the data base is fixed.

4.2 An Example

We are now in a position to present our example data base and formalize it at the information level.

The example data base is defined by a theory $T1 = (L1, A1)$, where $L1$ is a many-sorted temporal language with two sorts, *course* and *student*, and two predicate symbols, **offered,** of sort ⟨course⟩, and **takes,** of sort ⟨student, course⟩. The intended interpretation of **offered** (c) is that course c is offered, and of **takes**(s, c) is that student s takes course c. The set $A1$ of axioms consists of two formulas:

1) $\sim\exists s \exists c\ (\mathbf{takes}(s, c) \land \sim\mathbf{offered}(c))$
2) $\sim\exists s \exists c\ (\diamond(\mathbf{takes}(s, c) \land \diamond(\sim\exists c' \mathbf{takes}\ (s, c'))))$

The first formula formalizes the static constraint: "a student cannot take a course that is not being offered". The second formula formalizes the transition constraint: "the number of courses taken by a student cannot drop to zero" (i.e., he cannot be taking a course in (some) current state and no course in a future state).

To summarize, formalisms based on logic are best viewed as tools to describe data bases at the first level of specification since the set of consistent data base states and the set of consistent state transitions can be formalized by sets of axioms.

5 The Functions Level – The Use of Algebraic Formalisms

Recall that the goal of a second level specification is to define a set of query and update functions that preserve the static and transition constraints listed at the first-level specification, provided that only such functions be used (the *encapsulation* strategy). This can be achieved by giving the data base application an algebraic specification [VF, DMW].

At the functions level, a data base is still specified as a first-order theory T2 = (L2, A2). However, the similarities with a first-level specification fade out with a closer look at T2.

5.1 Algebraic Formalisms

An algebraic specification is a first-order theory T = (L, A), where L is a many-sorted first-order language and A is a set of axioms obeying the following restrictions.

The set of sorts of L must include a *Boolean* sort and a designated sort *state* (also called *sort-of-interest*). The remaining sorts are called *parameter sorts.* The only predicate symbols of L are equality symbols of sort ⟨s, s⟩, for each sort s. For simplicity, and since no ambiguity arises, they are all denoted by "=". We shall also use $t \neq t'$ as an abbreviation for $\sim(t = t')$. The parameter sorts of L are endowed with their own function symbols (not involving the sort *state* either as a domain or range sort, and not including *Boolean* as domain sort) which have the effect of generating a set of ground terms called *parameter names.*

The *Boolean* sort will be equipped with two constants, *True* and *False*, and with function symbols standing for the usual connectives, $\sim$, $\wedge$, $\vee$, $\rightarrow$, $\equiv$ written in infix notation.

The language L may also have other function symbols as long as *state* occurs as one of the domain sorts and the range sort is *Boolean* or *state.* To simplify the notation, we assume that *state* is always the last one in the list of domain sorts. Thus, if f is an n-ary function symbol in this group, it must have a sort of the form ⟨s1, ..., sn-1, *state*, sn + 1⟩ (recall that sn + 1 is the target sort). If sn + 1 is the sort *state* then f is *update function* (intuitively, it maps states into states according to some arguments); otherwise, f is a *query function* (it interrogates the current state (according to some arguments) and returns a value). Let f be an n-ary query function. Whenever terms of sorts other than *state* are irrelevant, we will write $f(\sigma)$ instead of $f(t1, \ldots, tn-1, \sigma)$.

A term of the form q(t1, ..., tn) where q is a query function and t1, ..., tn contain no occurrences of update functions is called a *simple observation*. We will construct the language L2 to be sufficiently rich with queries so that states can be identified by means of simple observations. More precisely, if σ and σ' are state variables such that for all simple observations f we have $f(\sigma)=f(\sigma')$, then $\sigma=\sigma'$. This *observability condition* is often fulfilled by data base applications due to their purpose.

The type of axioms allowed in algebraic specifications will be *conditional equations*, which are wffs of the form $P \rightarrow t=t'$ where P is a wff and t and t' are terms of the same sort s. If s is *state* then we call the axiom an *U-equation*, otherwise we call the axiom a *Q-equation*. Often term t' is "simpler" than t and we can view an axiom as a conditional term-rewriting rule, namely, if condition c is fulfilled then t can be rewritten as t'. This operational interpretation has an intuitive appeal to it, which can be conveniently exploited.

An algebraic specification, being a theory, defines a set of structures, the models of the theory. (In the context of algebraic specifications, structures are called (many-sorted) algebras.) As usual, we further restrict this set to be the set of all *finitely generated algebras* (i.e., those in which every element is the value of a variable-free term) which are models of the axioms. Thus we can employ the principle of structural induction (on terms) as a proof rule.

We call an algebraic specification $T=(L,A)$ *sufficiently complete* iff for every ground term of the form q(t1, ..., tn), where q is a query function (with target sort s, say), there exists a parameter name p (of sort s) such that $A \models q(t1, \ldots, tn) = p$. Intuitively, a sufficiently complete algebraic specification is one enabling the evaluation of all queries.

Returning to the beginning of our discussion, we can concisely say that data base applications are specified at the functions level by algebraic specifications. The next section outlines in general terms the methodology to obtain such data base specifications.

5.2 Obtaining a Functions Level Specification – An Example

We now outline the methodology we employ to obtain an algebraic specification $T2=(L2, A2)$ of a data base application at the functions level.

Consider again the data base application described at the information level by the theory $T1=(L1,A1)$ of Sect. 4.2. For simplicity, we take the parameter sorts of L2 as the sorts of L1. Moreover, we correlate the db-predicate symbols of L1 describing data base structures with query function δ symbols. So, L2 will contain two query function symbols, *offered* and *takes*, of sorts ⟨course, state, Boolean⟩ and ⟨student, course, state, Boolean⟩, respectively. The intended interpretation of *offered* (c, σ), for example, is that it is *True* iff c is a course offered in state σ.

The update function symbols (with their intended interpretation) are: *initiate* of sort ⟨state⟩, with *initiate* understood as an operation that initializes the data base;

offer of sort ⟨course, state, state⟩, where *offer* $(c, \sigma) = \tau$ indicates that c is added as a new course to state σ, creating state τ; *cancel* of sort ⟨course, state, state⟩, where *cancel* $(c, \sigma) = \tau$ means the inverse of the previous operation; *enroll* of sort ⟨student, course, state, state⟩, where *enroll* $(s, c, \sigma) = \tau$ creates a new state τ by enrolling student s to course c on state σ; *transfer* of sort ⟨student, course, course, state, state⟩, with *transfer* $(s, c, c', \sigma) = \tau$ understood as creating state τ from state σ by transferring student s from course c to course c'.

Our task now is to write a set of conditional equations from which we can obtain the correct result of every query and, at the same time, guarantee that consistency is always preserved. In other words, for every query function q, for all parameters p and for all ground terms t of sort *state*, we should be able to derive from the axioms the equality $q(p, t) = b$ where the *Boolean* value b is the correct answer according to the given description. Now, the set T of ground terms of sort *state* is the smallest set of terms containing *initiate* and closed under symbolic application of the other update functions. Thus, we shall strive for Q-equations of the form (perhaps with some condition)

$q(p, u(p', \sigma)) =$ "simpler expression"

for all query functions q, update functions u and parameter lists p and p', σ being a variable of sort *state*.

We start from the informal description of the operations. As already mentioned the effect of each update function is changing the state as observed by the query functions. As a first step, we give a more structured description for each update function by identifying its *intended effects*, *preconditions* for state change, possible *side effects*, and simple observations that are *not affected*.
The general outlook of such a structured description by means of effects for an update u is

$\tau = u$ (parameters, σ)

intended effects:	some simple observations q at state τ give specific values
pre-conditions:	some simple observations q' at state σ have given values
side effects:	some simple observations $\hat{q}$ may have their values altered by passing from state σ to state τ
not-affected:	other simple observations q'' maintain at state τ the value they had at state σ

For example, the informal description of the update function *cancel* would be structured as follows

$\tau =$ *cancel* (c, σ)
/* course c is cancelled at τ, provided that no student is taking it at state σ */

intended effects:	*offered* $(c, \tau) =$ *False*
pre-conditions:	$\forall$s (*takes* $(s, c, \sigma) =$ *False*)
side-effects:	none
not-affected:	all other queries, including *offered* (c', .) with $c' \neq c$

As an example of the method, let us consider the update function *cancel*, whose structured effects description has been given above. We shall examine in detail the case of the query *offered*. In other words, we want (conditional) equations enabling us to derive the correct results of queries of the form

$$offered\ (c', cancel\ (c, \sigma))$$

We shall divide our task into two cases depending on the comparison of c′ with c.

For the first case (c′ ≠ c) the not-affected part of the structured description tells that the value of *offered* (c′, .) is not affected by the update, i.e.

$$offered\ (c', cancel\ (c, \sigma)) = offered\ (c', \sigma)$$

We can put this into the form of a conditional equation

$$c' \neq c \rightarrow offered\ (c', cancel\ (c, \sigma)) = offered\ (c', \sigma)$$

Notice that the antecedent of the conditional equation does not involve terms of sort *state*, only parameters. Also, the righthand side of the consequent is "simpler" than its lefthand side, for the term σ is "simpler" than the term *cancel* (c, σ). Thus, we can view this conditional equation as reducing the problem of determining the value of *offered* (c′, *cancel* (c, σ)) to the simpler problem of determining *offered* (c′, σ) in case c′ ≠ c.

Now let us examine the case c′ = c. According to the structured description, the value of *offered* (c, *cancel* (c, σ)) will depend on the precondition. If the precondition holds then we have the intended effect *False*. Otherwise the value remains unchanged. Thus, we have:

$$offered\ (c, cancel\ (c, \sigma)) =$$

$$\begin{array}{ll} False & \text{if } \forall s\ (takes\ (s, c, \sigma) = False) \\ offered\ (c, \sigma) & \text{if } \exists s\ (takes\ (s, c, \sigma) = True) \end{array}$$

Now, in view of the static constraint, we have

$$\exists s\ (takes\ (s, c, \sigma) = True) \rightarrow offered\ (c, \sigma) = True$$

So, we can write

$$offered\ (c, cancel\ (c, \sigma)) =$$

$$\begin{array}{ll} False & \text{if } (\exists s\ takes\ (s, c, \sigma)) = False \\ True & \text{if } (\exists s\ takes\ (s, c, \sigma)) = True \end{array}$$

which can be simplified to

$$offered\ (c, cancel\ (c, \sigma)) = True \equiv \exists s\ (takes\ (c, c, \sigma) = True)$$

This wff can be rewritten as two conditional equations:

$$\exists s\ (takes\ (s, c, \sigma) = True) \rightarrow offered\ (c, cancel\ (c, \sigma)) = True$$

and

$$\sim \exists s\ (takes\ (s, c, \sigma) = True) \rightarrow offered\ (c, cancel\ (c, \sigma)) = False$$

Three remarks are in order. First, in obtaining this equation we used the static constraint (assumed to hold; we shall later have to verify that it does hold). Second, the antecedents of the above conditional equations do not involve quantification over states, only over parameters. Third, we may regard these equations as reducing the problem of determining *offered* (c, *cancel* (c, σ)) to that of determining whether there exists a student s such that *takes* (s, c, σ) = *True*, which may be viewed as a problem somewhat simpler than the original one. However we must be careful, for some other equation might reduce the problem of determining *takes* (s, c, σ) to that of determining *offered* (c, σ), thereby creating a circularity. This is the reason why we later verify termination.

By applying the general methodology outlined above we obtain the following set of Q-equations for our example

1. $\mathit{offered}\ (c,\ \mathit{initiate}) = \mathit{False}$
2. $\mathit{takes}\ (s, c,\ \mathit{initiate}) = \mathit{False}$
3. $\mathit{offered}\ (c,\ \mathit{offer}\ (c, \sigma)) = \mathit{True}$
4. $c \neq c' \rightarrow \mathit{offered}\ (c,\ \mathit{offer}\ (c', \sigma)) = \mathit{offered}\ (c, \sigma)$
5. $\mathit{takes}\ (s, c,\ \mathit{offer}\ (c', \sigma)) = \mathit{takes}\ (s, c, \sigma)$
6. $\mathit{offered}\ (c,\ \mathit{cancel}\ (c, \sigma)) = \mathit{True} \equiv \exists s\ (\mathit{takes}\ (s, c, \sigma) = \mathit{True})$
7. $c \neq c' \rightarrow \mathit{offered}\ (c,\ \mathit{cancel}\ (c', \sigma)) = \mathit{offered}\ (c, \sigma)$
8. $\mathit{takes}\ (s, c,\ \mathit{cancel}\ (c', \sigma)) = \mathit{takes}\ (s, c, \sigma)$
9. $\mathit{offered}\ (c,\ \mathit{enroll}\ (s, c', \sigma)) = \mathit{offered}\ (c, \sigma)$
10. $\mathit{takes}\ (s, c,\ \mathit{enroll}\ (s, c, \sigma)) = \mathit{offered}\ (c, \sigma)$
11. $s \neq s' \vee c \neq c' \rightarrow \mathit{takes}\ (s, c,\ \mathit{enroll}\ (s', c', \sigma)) = \mathit{takes}\ (s, c, \sigma)$
12. $\mathit{offered}\ (c,\ \mathit{transfer}\ (s, c', c'', \sigma)) = \mathit{offered}\ (c, \sigma)$
13. $\mathit{takes}\ (s, c',\ \mathit{transfer}\ (s, c, c', \sigma)) = (\mathit{offered}\ (c', \sigma) \wedge \mathit{takes}\ (s, c, \sigma)) \vee \mathit{takes}\ (s, c', \sigma)$
14. $\mathit{takes}\ (s, c,\ \mathit{transfer}\ (s, c, c', \sigma)) = (\sim \mathit{offered}\ (c', \sigma) \vee \mathit{takes}\ (s, c', \sigma)) \wedge \mathit{takes}\ (s, c, \sigma)$
15. $s \neq s' \vee (c \neq c' \wedge c \neq c'') \rightarrow \mathit{takes}\ (s, c,\ \mathit{transfer}\ (s', c', c'', \sigma)) = \mathit{takes}\ (s, c, \sigma)$

5.3 First to Second Level Refinements

The information and functions level specifications of a data base application are bound by a notion of refinement we describe in this section.

Let T1 = (L1, A1) and T2 = (L2, A2) be the information and functions level specifications of the data base application. Intuitively, we say that T2 *refines* T1 iff all equations in A2 are sufficient to guarantee that all updates preserve consistency with respect to the static and transition constraints in A1. Although this condition is on the surface simple, it creates some technical difficulties to be formalized, mainly because the two languages, L1 and L2, are of different types. In particular, wffs of L1 may contain modalities, which are not part of L2.

For simplicity, we assume that every sort of L1 is a parameter sort of L2 and every variable of sort s is also a variable of L2. Of course L2 has two new sorts, *state* and *Boolean*, as well as new variables ranging over them.

The notion of refinement is formally defined by specifying an *interpretation* I mapping the non-logical symbols of L1 into terms and wffs of L2 with the following characteristics:

1) for each n-ary db-predicate symbol r of sort ⟨s1, ..., sn⟩ of L1, I(r) must be a term of L2 of sort *Boolean* and free variables x1, ..., xn, y of sorts s1, ..., sn, *state*
2) for each other n-ary predicate symbol p of sort ⟨s1, ..., sn⟩ of L1, I(p) must be a wff of L2 with free variables x1, ..., xn of sorts s1, ..., sn
3) for each function symbol f of sort ⟨s1, ..., sn, sn + 1⟩ of L1, I(f) must be a term of L2 of sort sn + 1 and free variables x1, ..., xn of sorts s1, ..., sn

In our running example, we might define an interpretation I that assigns to the db-predicate symbol **offered** the term *offered* (c, σ) and to **takes** the term *takes* (s, c, σ).

Thus, the notion of interpretation defined above follows closely the idea of first-order interpretation. The differences are basically that some symbols of L1 are associated with terms of sort *Boolean* of L2, and not wffs of L2 as one would expect, and the addition of new sorts (and variables).

If t is a term of L2 with free variables x1, ..., xn of sorts s1, ..., sn and t1, ..., tn are terms of L2 also of sorts s1, ..., sn, let t [t1/x1, ..., tn/xn] denote the term of L2 obtained by replacing xi by ti, i = 1, ..., n.

Given an interpretation I, we extend I to map wffs of L1 into wffs of L2. However, in order to do so, we must extend L2 by adding a predicate symbol F of sort t ⟨state, state⟩, which will stand for the reachability relation R of the semantics of L1. The extension of I is defined as follows:

1) for any wff P of L1, I(P) = (∀sJ(s, P)), where s is a variable of sort *state* of L2

The mapping J in turn maps pairs (s, P), where s is a variable of L2 of sort *state* and P is a wff of L1, into wffs of L2. J is defined as follows:

2) J(s, x) = x, if x is a variable of L1
3) J(s, f(t1, ..., tn)) = I(f) [J(s, t1)/x1, ..., J(s, tn)/xn], if f is a function symbol of L1
4) J(s, p(t1, ..., tn)) = I(p) [J(s, t1)/x1, ..., J(s, tn)/xn], if p is a predicate symbol of L1 (other than a db-predicate symbol)
5) J(s, r(t1, ..., tn) = I(r) [J(s, t1)/x1, ..., J(s, tn)/xn, s/y] = *True* if r is a db-predicate symbol
6) J(s, ~P) = ~J(s, P)
7) J(s, P1 ∧ P2) = J(s, P1) ∧ J(s, P2)
8) J(s, ∃xP) = ∃xJ(s, P)
9) J(s, □P) = ∀s′(F(s, s′) → J(s′, P)), where s′ is a variable of L2 of sort state not used before
10) J(s, ◇P) = ∃s′(F(s, s′) ∧ J(s′, P)), where s′ is a variable of L2 of sort state not used before

Thus, at this point we know how to map wffs of L1 into wffs of L2. Therefore, we can check if indeed the axioms of T2 are enough to guarantee that all updates of T2 preserve consistency. More precisely, we say that T2 is a *correct refinement* of T1 under a given interpretation I iff for any axiom P of T1, I(P) is a theorem of T2.

As for first-order languages, our notion of interpretation can also be used to induce a mapping from structures of L2 into universes of L1, which permits us to give an alternative (semantical) characterization of correct refinement. Indeed, given an interpretation I from L1 into L2, we define a mapping M from structures of L2, which must be finitely generated algebras by assumption, into universes of L1 as follows.

Let A be a structure of L2 and assume that A is finitely generated. Extend A to assign meaning to the predicate symbol F added to L2 as follows:
$(e, e') \in A(F)$ iff there exists a term $t(\sigma)$ of L2 of sort *state*, whose only variable is σ also of sort *state*, such that

$$\models A(t(\sigma) = \sigma')\,[e/\sigma, e'/\sigma']$$

where σ' is another variable of sort *state*. Intuitively, e′ is F-related to e in A iff some trace constructing e′ will pass by e′ will pass by e as an intermediate step.

Then, M(A) = (S, R) is the universe of L1 induced by A, where S is a set of structures for L1 differing only on the values of the db-predicate symbols of L1 and R is a binary relation over S. The set S is defined by taking each element e in the domain of A of sort *state* and constructing a structure E of L1 as follows:

1) for each sort s of L1, the domain of E of sort s is the domain of A of sort s
2) if f is a function symbol of L1 of sort $\langle s1, \ldots, sn, sn+1\rangle$, E(f) is the function defined by I(f) in A, that is,

   $E(f) = \{(a1, \ldots, an, b)/A(I(f))\,(a1, \ldots, an) = b\}$

3) if p is a predicate symbol of L1 of sort $\langle s1, \ldots, sn\rangle$, E(p) is the relation defined by I(p) in A, that is,

   $E(p) = A(I(p))$

4) if r is a db-predicate symbol of L1 of sort $\langle s1, \ldots, sn\rangle$, E(r) is the relation defined by I(r) and e, the element of the domain of A of sort state associated with E, that is,

   $E(r) = \{(a1, \ldots, an)/A(I(r))\,(a1, \ldots, an, e) = A(\mathit{True})\}$

The relation R is in turn defined as follows:

5) (E, E′) is in R iff (e, e′) is in A(F) where e, e′ are the elements of the domain of A of sort *state* associated with E and E′, respectively.

We can prove one basic property of M. We say that a wff P of L1 is *valid* in a universe U = (S, R) of L1 iff P is valid in every structure E in S. Also, we call U a *model* of a set W of wffs iff every wff in W is valid in U.

Theorem 4.1: For any wff P of L1 and any structure A of L2, P is valid in M(A) iff I(P) is valid in A.

As a consequence of this theorem, we have an alternative definition of correct refinement:

Theorem 4.2: T2 is a correct refinement of T1 under a given interpretation I iff for any model A of T2, M(A) is a model of T1, where M is the mapping induced by I.

In addition to the above result, the notion of refinement also has a second semantic interpretation. Assume that T2 is a correct refinement of T1. Then, T2 in fact refines the semantic specification of the data base by explicitly defining the reachability relation R in terms of the repeated application of update operations (which is the meaning assigned to the function symbol F).

5.4 Proof of Correctness of the Refinement – An Example

Let T2 = (L2, A2) be the algebraic specification of the data base application obtained in Sect. 5.2. We must guarantee that T2 has the following properties:

- it is sufficiently complete and correct with respect to the structured description;
- it is a refinement of the first-level specification given in Sect. 4.2.

By construction our equations are already correct with respect to the structured description. We proceed by proving:

a) sufficient completeness
b) static consistency, i.e. every reachable state is valid
c) transition consistency

Parts b) and c) are equivalent to saying that the refinement is correct.
We outline below how these properties can be proven.

a) Sufficient Completeness

We can view our set of Q-equations as a system of mutually recursive equations defining the query functions. From this viewpoint, sufficient completeness amounts to termination of this system of recursive definitions. There are several criteria for checking termination of such term rewriting systems. However, the basic idea is checking the absence of circularity in these definitions. This basic idea will do for cases simple as our example, as we now illustrate.

We consider a graph whose nodes are the terms occurring in the equations disregarding their parameters. For each equation with term t0 on its lefthand side and t1, ..., tn on its righthand side we draw directed edges from the node corresponding to t0 to those corresponding to t1, ..., tn. For instance, Eq. 6 and 7 will contribute the following partial graph

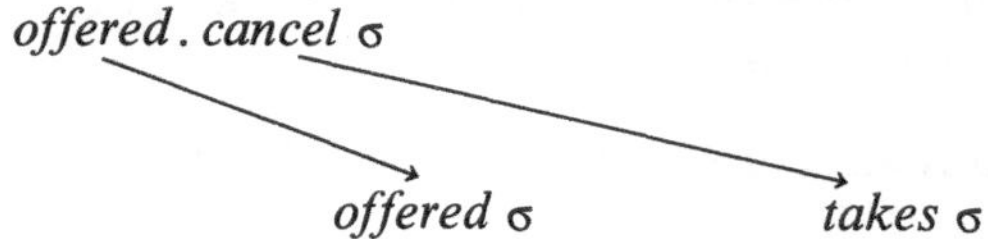

The graph for our example will have 12 nodes and 14 edges. It is easy to check that it has no cycles. Since this graph has no cycles it corresponds to a well-founded relation on ground queries. Therefore, the recursive definitions do terminate.

b) Every Reachable State is Valid

Consider the set V of all *valid states*, i.e. the set defined by

$\forall c \forall s\,(takes\ (s, c, \sigma) = True \rightarrow offered\ (c, \sigma) = True)$

The set G of *reachable states* is the least set of states containing the value of *initiate* and closed under all the other update functions. So in order to show that the static constraint is satisfied at the functions level, i.e. $G \subseteq V$, it suffices to show that V contains *initiate* and is closed under all the other update functions.

Clearly, by Eq. 2, *initiate* is in V. To show that V is closed under applications of *cancel*, we have to check that *cancel* $(c', \sigma) \in V$ whenever $\sigma \in V$. For this purpose we have to show that for all courses c and students s if *takes* (s, c, *cancel* (c', σ)) = *True* then *offered* (c, *cancel* (c', σ)) = *True*. We consider two cases:

case 1: $c \neq c'$

Then, by Eq. 7 and 8, we have

offered (c, *cancel* (c', σ)) = *offered* (c, σ)
takes (s, c, *cancel* (c', σ)) = *takes* (s, c, σ)

whence, as $\sigma \in V$, we have the desired implication.

case 2: $c = c'$

Then, by Eq. 6,

offered (c, *cancel* (c', σ)) = *True* ≡ ∃s′ *takes* (s′, c, σ) = *True*

This suggests considering two subcases according to the value of *takes* (s, c, σ). First, in case *takes* (s, c, σ) = *True*, then

∃s′ *takes* (s′, c, σ) = *True*, so

offered (c, *cancel* (c′, σ)) = *True*

On the other hand, if *takes* (s, c, σ) = *False*, then, by Eq. 8 we obtain

takes (s, c, *cancel* (c, σ)) = *takes* (s, c, σ) = *False*

Therefore, the implication always holds and we can conclude *cancel* $(c', \sigma) \in V$.

By proceeding similarly with the other update functions and invoking the appropriate equations we check the closure of V, whence $G \subseteq V$.

Notice that we have illustrated with our example a perfectly general method to show that the functions level of a data base application given by an algebraic specification satisfies the declared static constraints. Namely, by invoking the equations show that the set of all valid states is closed under all update functions (including constants), which can be done syntactically, as above.

c) Transition Consistency

The transition constraint of our example (see Sect. 3.2) is logically equivalent to

$\forall s \forall c\, [\diamond(\textit{takes}\,(s, c) \rightarrow \square(\exists c'\, \textit{takes}\,(s, c')))]$

which can be rewritten, by applying the notion of refinement as

$\forall \sigma 0 \{\forall s \forall c \forall \sigma [F(\sigma 0, \sigma) \rightarrow [\textit{takes}\,(s, c, \sigma) = \textit{True} \rightarrow \forall \tau (F(\sigma, \tau) \rightarrow \exists c'\, \textit{takes}\,(s, c', \tau) = \textit{True})]]\}$

where F corresponds to the accessibility relation.
We shall first check

$$\forall s \forall c \forall \sigma\, [\mathit{takes}(s, c, \sigma) = \mathit{True} \rightarrow \exists c'\ \mathit{takes}(s, c', u(\sigma)) = \mathit{True}]$$

for each update function u other than *initiate*.

We illustrate this checking with the case of *cancel*. For this purpose, notice that, by Eq. 8

$$\mathit{takes}\ (s, c', \mathit{cancel}\ (c'', \sigma)) = \mathit{takes}\ (s, c', \sigma).$$

So, if *takes* $(s, c, \sigma) = \mathit{True}$ then there exists $c' = c$ such that *takes* $(s, c', \mathit{cancel}\ (c'', \sigma)) = \mathit{True}$.

The case of *offer* is entirely similar. For the update functions *enroll* and *transfer* the checking can be performed by breaking into cases depending on the comparison of the values of the parameters.

Thus we have that every single-update transition obeys the transition constraint. It follows readily, by induction, that every transition (effected by a sequence of updates) also obeys the transition constraint.

6 The Representation Level – The Use of a Programming Language Formalism

As the name indicates, the representation phase, the last phase of the specification process, provides a representation of the objects of the data base and a description of the functions using some appropriate language. However, since we remain at the specification level, the representation of the objects should be based on abstract data structures, such as those underlying the current *data models*, and the functions should be programmed as procedures written in a programming language supporting the data structures of the data model. Moreover, the programming language should be simple and theoretically sound and must be formally specified so as to permit verifying if the procedures indeed realize the functions.

We note that, by specifying a language associated with a data model, we are in a sense providing a formal specification of the data model itself.

6.1 Programming Language Formalism

This section describes the syntax and semantics of what we call a data base schema at the representation level. The language to be used, *RPR*, is based on an extension of the concept of regular programs over relations described in [CB], to which the reader is referred for a fuller discussion.

6.1.1 Syntax – The Use of a Grammatical Formalism

Briefly, the syntax of a data base schema is defined as follows. Let L be a many-sorted first-order language with a set of distinguished constants, called *scalar program variables*. If P is a wff of L with free variables x1, ..., xm, then we call an expression of the form {(x1, ..., xm)/P} a *relational term* of type ⟨s1, ..., sm⟩, if si is the type of xi.

A data base schema has the following format:

schema SCL; OPL end-schema

SCL is a list of statements of the form R(A1, ..., An) where R is a predicate symbol of L and A1, ..., An are unary predicate symbols of L such that, if ⟨s1, ..., sn⟩ is the sort of R, then Ai has sort ⟨si⟩, for each i = 1, ..., n. Each predicate symbol R in SCL is called a *relation name* or *relational program variable*. OPL is a list of *operation declarations* of the form 'proc I(Y1, ..., Yn) = S' where I is an *operation identifier*, Yi is either a scalar or a relational program variable, and S is a statement, called the *operation body*.

The set of statements (based on L), is defined inductively as follows:

1) For any scalar program variable x of L and any variable-free term t of L of the same type as x, the expression x := t is an *assignment statement*.
2) For any relational program variable R of L and any relational term F of the same type as R, the expression R := F is a *relational assignment statement*.
3) For any closed wff P of L, P? is a *test statement*.
4) For any statements p and q, the expressions (p ∪ q), (p; q) and p* are statements called the *union* of p and q, the *composition* of p and q and the *iteration* of p, respectively.

We may also introduce some familiar constructs by definition as follows:

5) if P then r else s = (P?; r) ∪ (~P?; s)
6) if P then r = (P?; r) ∪ ~P?
7) while P do r = (P?; r)*; ~P? ∪ ~P?
8) insert R(x1, ..., xn) = R := {(y1, ..., yn)/R(y1, ..., yn) ∨ (y1 = x1 ∧ ... ∧ yn = xn)}
9) delete R(x1, ..., xn) = R := {(y1, ..., yn)/R(y1, ..., yn) ∧ ~(y1 = x1 ∧ ... ∧ yn = xn)}

If we use only the constructs in 5) to 9) in lieu of 3) and 4) we obtain the set of *deterministic programs*.

The formal definition of the syntax of data base schemas is given using W-grammars (see also [FVC]). W-grammars (as also other comparable formalisms, such as attribute grammars and affix grammars) go beyond BNF in that they can express context-sensitive restrictions (e.g. that all relational program variables in the OPL part of a schema have been declared in the SCL part), and can be used to build compiler generators. A correspondence between W-grammars and logic has been established in [He].

A *W-grammar* is an 8-tuple G = (M, S, T, z, MT, H, RM, RH), where

- M is a finite set of *metanotions* (which are denoted by sequences of capital letters);
- S is a finite set of *s-notions* (which are denoted by sequences of lower-case letters);
- T is a finite set of *terminals* (which are denoted by sequences of lower-case letters between double quotes (following [Pe]) or by indicated special symbols);
- z in S+ is the *start symbol*;
- MT ⊂ S is a set of *metaterminals*;
- H ⊂ (M ∪ S)+ is a set of *hypernotions*;
- RM ⊂ M x(M ∪ MT)* is a finite set of *metarules* (which are written as X0 : : X1 X2 ... Xm.);
- RH ⊂ H x(H ∪ T)* is a set of *hyperrules* (which are written in the form x0: x1, x2, ..., xn.).

Notes:

1) Sets M, S and T are pairwise disjoint;
2) Metarules with the same left-hand side may be combined using '|' to separate the right-hand side alternatives; the same convention also applies to hyperrules. The null sequence is denoted by '&'.

By applying metarules just like ordinary context-free rules, one can generate from a metanotion X sequences of metaterminals called *metaproductions* of X. Here, the *language generated by a metanotion X*, L(X), consists of all metaproductions derived from X by such production rules.

Consider a hyperrule x0 : x1, ..., xk.. Since each xi is an element of (M ∪ S)+, it may contain occurrences of X. By taking a metaproduction y of X and consistently replacing each occurrence of X in the hyperrule by y we obtain a new rule x0′ : x1′, x2′, ..., xk′.. If we perform this process of *uniform replacement* on all metanotions occurring in the hyperrule we obtain the context-free production rule x0″ : x1″, x2″, ..., xk″. where each xi″ is a sequence without metanotions. The *language generated by a hypernotion h*, L(h), consists of all sequences of terminals derived from h by such production rules and the language generated by the W-grammar G is L(z).
Whenever possible, a W-grammar will be defined by exhibiting just its meta and hyperrules, leaving implicit the other elements of the grammar.

We now turn to the definition of the syntax of RPR. To simplify the discussion, we assume that we are given a many-sorted first-order language L whose syntax is defined by a W-grammar GL with the following metanotions:

- V such that L(V) is the set of variables of L;
- P such that L(P) is the set of predicate symbols of L;
- R such that L(R) is a set of distinguished predicate symbols of L (these will be called *relational program variables*);
- F such that L(F) is the set of function symbols of L;
- X such that L(X) is a set of distinguished constants (0-ary function symbols) of L (these will be called *scalar program variables*);
- T such that L(T) is the set of terms of L;
- W such that L(W) is the set of wffs of L;

and, for each w in L(W) and each list $\hat{x}$ of variables, the hypernotions below (These are cases of what is called a *predicate* in the W-grammar terminology. We say that a predicate succeeds if through the application of appropriate production rules, it eventually vanishes (i.e. the symbol & is generated); otherwise a *blind alley* situation is reached.):

- 'where w is closed' such that L (where w is closed) is {&} if w is a closed wff, and ϕ otherwise;
- 'where {$\hat{x}$/w} is well formed' such that L (where {$\hat{x}$/w} is well formed) = {&} if $\hat{x}$ is a list of all variables that occur free in w and is ϕ otherwise;

and, for each n-ary relational program variable R and for each list A1, ..., An of unary predicate symbols, the following hypernotion:

- 'where A1, ..., An matches r' such that L (where A1, ..., An matches R) is {&}, if Ai is of sort ⟨Ti⟩, $1 \leqq i \leqq n$, and R is of sort ⟨T1, ..., Tn⟩, and is ϕ otherwise;

and, for each n-ary program variable R, each relational term E and each list of schemes SCL, the following hypernotion:

- 'where E relational program variables are in SCL' such that L (where E relational program variables are in SCL) is {&}, if each program variable appearing in E also appears (i.e. has been declared in SCL) and is ϕ otherwise; for the transformation of the hypernotion into {&}, the *general predicate* 'where ... contains ... ' [Pe] will be applied to check if each relational program variable R encountered in E is contained in SCL (notice a similar application of the same general predicate in the last hyperrule of the W-grammar below);

and, for each term t (relational or not) and each program variable x (relational or scalar), the following hypernotions:

- 'where t is ground' such that L (where t is ground) = {&}, if t is a ground term, and ϕ otherwise.
- 'where t agrees with x' such that L (where t agrees with x) is {&} if t and x are of the same type and ϕ otherwise.

This concludes what we assume about the W-grammar GL. The W-grammar defining the syntax of data base schemas is shown below (the start symbol is p, the first hyperrule to be invoked being indicated by '⇒').

Metarules

First-Order Objects
  (inherited from W-grammar GL)
Auxiliary objects

```
/*
  for each i = 1, ..., p
*/
I    :: I1 |...| Ik.            /* identifiers                */
E    :: {VL/W}.                 /* relational terms           */
Y    :: X | R.                  /* generic program variable   */
F    :: T | E.                  /* generic term               */
YL   :: Y   YL | &.             /* list of generic variables  */
FL   :: F   FL | &.             /* list of generic terms      */
VL   :: V   VL | V.             /* list of variables          */
```

First-Order Rules
  (inherited from GL)
Programming-Language Rules

```
/*
```

```
  context-free aspects of the syntax of RPR
*/
Q    :: schema SCL; OPL end-schema.   /* schema declaration      */
SCL  :: RL; SCL | RL.                 /* list of schemes         */
RL   :: R(PL).                        /* schemes definition      */
PL   :: P; PL | P.                    /* list of attributes      */
OPL  :: OP; OPL | OP.                 /* list of operations      */
OP   :: proc I (FL) = S.              /* operation declaration   */
S    :: S; S | S ∪ S | S* |           /* statements              */
          W? | X := T | R := E.
```

Hyperrules

First-Order Rules

```
  (inherited from GL essentially to define closed wffs and relational terms)
c : W, where W is closed.   /* L(c) is the set of all closed wffs */
g : T, where T is ground.   /* L(g) is the set of all ground (variable-free) terms */
```

Programming Language Rules

```
⇒ p : repr Q, where Q defined.
  /*
    terminal representation of programs –
    metaterminals are enclosed in quotes
  */
  repr schema SCL; OPL end-schema:
      "schema", repr SCL, ";", repr OPL, "end-schema".
  .                         /* further rules enclosing syntactical objects
  .                            within quotes    */
  repr & : &.
  /*
    checking procedure declarations and other statements
  */
  where schema SCL; OPL end-schema defined:
        where SCL defined,
        where ⟨SCL⟩ OPL defined.
  where R[PL] SCL defined      : where PL matches R,
                                 where SCL defined.
  where ⟨SCL⟩ proc I (YL) = S; OPL defined:
                                 where ⟨SCL⟩ S defined,
                                 where ⟨SCL⟩ OPL defined.
  where ⟨SCL⟩ & defined        : &.
  where ⟨SCL⟩ S1; S2 defined   : where ⟨SCL⟩ S1 defined,
                                 where ⟨SCL⟩ S2 defined.
  where ⟨SCL⟩ S1 ∪ S2 defined  : where ⟨SCL⟩ S1 defined,
                                 where ⟨SCL⟩ S2 defined.
  where ⟨SCL⟩ S* defined       : where ⟨SCL⟩ S defined.
  where ⟨SCL⟩ W? defined       : where W is closed,
        where W relational program variables are in SCL.
```

where ⟨SCL⟩ X := T defined : where T agrees with X,
where T is ground.
where ⟨SCL⟩ R := E defined : where E agrees with R,
where SCL contains R,
where E relational program variables are in SCL.

6.1.2 Semantics – The Use of a Denotational Formalism

Again, let us briefly discuss the semantics of data base schemas before giving the formal definitions.

Let L be the underlying many-sorted first-order language. For a given structure A of L and a given non-logical symbol s of L, let A(s) denote the value of s in A. Likewise, let A(t) be the value of a variable-free term t of L in A and let A(F) be the relation denoted by F, if F is a relational term.

A *universe* U for L is a set of structures of L satisfying three conditions:

(i) any two structures in U differ only on the values of the scalar or relational program variables;
(ii) for any A in U, any scalar program variable x and any element e of the domain of the sort of x, there is B in U such that A and B differ only on the value of x, which is e in B;
(iii) for any A in U, any relational program variable R of sort (s1, ..., sn) and any n-ary relation $r \subset Ds1 \times \ldots \times Dsn$, where Dsi is the domain of sort si, there is B in U such that A and B differ only on the value of R, which is r in B.

These conditions guarantee that, for example, if the value of x is changed to e, the resulting structure is in U, that is, the universe is closed under assignment, so to speak. Note that, by (i), all structures in U have the same domain and the same value on all symbols, except on the scalar and relational program variables.

For a fixed universe U of L, the meaning of statements is given by a function m assigning to each statement in RPR a binary relation in U as follows:

1) m(x:=t) = {(A, B)/B is equal to A, except that B(x) = A(t)}
2) m(R:={(x1, ..., xn)/P}) = {(A, B)/B is equal to A, except that B(R) is the n-ary relation defined by P in A}
3) m(P?) = {(A, A)/P is true in A}
4) $m(p \cup q) = m(p) \cup m(q)$ (union of both binary relations)
5) m(p; q) = m(p). m(q) (composition of both binary relations)
6) m(p*) = (m(p))* (reflexive-transitive closure of m(p))

The meaning of procedure declarations is given by a function k assigning to each procedure declaration d of the form proc I (Y1, ..., Ym) = S a function from Ds1 x ... x Dsm into the set of all binary relations over the universe, where Dsi is the domain of type si and Yi is of type si. The function k is defined as follows:

7) k(d) = f iff for any (c1, ..., cm) in Ds1 x ... x Dsm, f(c1, ..., cm) is the set of all pairs (A, B) in UxU such that (A[c1/Y1, ..., cm/Ym], B) is in m(S).

We now sketch a formal definition of the semantics of data base schemas using the denotational approach. A certain familiarity with this approach at the level of, e.g. [Pa], is assumed.

The semantics will be specified by defining functions that assign to each element in a set of syntactical objects, called a *syntactical domain*, a value taken from a *semantic domain.*

Each syntactical domain will coincide with the language associated with a non-terminal of the W-grammar introduced in Sect. 6.1.1. For example, the language associated with V is the *domain of variables*. The table below lists all syntactical domains of interest. By convention, N:S indicates that S is the name of the syntactical domain associated with the non-terminal N, that is, of the language L(N) associated with N by the W-grammar.

Syntactical Domains

First-Order Domains

V : Var	variables
P : Pred	predicate symbols
F : Func	function symbols
T : Term	terms
g : G-term	variable-free (ground) terms
W : Wff	well-formed formulas (wffs)
c : C-wff	closed wffs

Programming-Language Domains

OP: Oper	operations
S : Stmt	statements
X : S-var	scalar program variables
R : R-var	relational program variables
E : R-term	relational terms
I : Iden	identifiers

Auxiliary Domains

Y : G-var	generic variables
F : G-term	generic terms
VL : L-var	list of variables

The semantic domains are defined in the next table. Some comments come in order before introducing the table, though. The notation v : S this time indicates that v is a variable (of the metatheory) taking values from the set S. As usual in the denotational approach, $\top$ and $\bot$ indicate "overdetermined" and "undetermined", respectively. The set ST consists of *states* or functions assigning a scalar value to each scalar program variable and relation to each relational program variable, respecting their types.

Semantic Domains

t : TR = {True, False}	truth values
vi: Dsi	a domain of values for type si including $\top$ and $\bot$
s : ST	a universe of states

The *semantic functions* are just five and are defined in the sequel. We have functions m and k, as discussed before, which are defined in terms of three other functions taken from first-order logic. We have a function A that is a structure with domain Ds1, ..., Dsm for the underlying first-order language L (with sorts s1, ..., sm), except that A does not assign meaning to the scalar or relational program variables (which are distinguished constants and predicte symbols of the language). These objects have their meaning fixed by a state. Or, putting it differently, a state s together with A determine a structure A(s) for L. We have a function I which, for each such structure A(s), acts as the interpretation of the closed formulas and variable-free terms of L based on A(s). Finally, we have a function J which, for each structure A(s), assigns a relation over the appropriate domains to each relational term.

The following notational conventions will be used. If o is a syntactical object and f is a semantic function, then f⟦o⟧ will denote the value of o assigned by f; if f: A → (B → C) is a semantic function, o is in A and q is in B, then we use f⟦o⟧ q to denote the value assigned to o and q by f; if s is a state, x is a scalar program variable of sort t and b is an element of the domain of t, then s[b/x] is the state that is equal to s, except that the value of x is b; likewise, s[r/R] denotes the state that is equal to s, except that the value of a relational program variable R is a relation r over the correct domains. Finally, if A and B are binary relations, then A . B, A ∪ B and A* denote the composition of A to B, the union of A and B and the reflexive and transitive closure of A, respectively, and xAy denotes a pair in A.

Semantic Functions and Equations

Semantic Functions

k : Oper → (∪(Ds → P(STx ST)))
  where s = (si1, ..., sij) ranges over the set of all sequences of types and Ds indicates Dsi1x ... xDsij, and where P(C) denotes the powerset of C

m: Stmt → P(STxST)

A: Pred ∪ Func → (∪(P(Ds)) ∪ ∪(Ds → Dsi))
  (same remark as above)

I : G-Term ∪ C-Wff → ST → (∪(Dsi) ∪ TR ∪ ∪(P(Ds)))
  (same remark as above)

J : R-Term → ST → ∪(P(Ds))
  (same remark as above)

Semantic Equations

First-Order Logic Equations

- for each s in ST, s ∪A is a structure for L, the underlying many-sorted first-order language
- for each s in ST, s ∪A induces an interpretation for L, which fixes the value of I⟦a⟧s when a is in G-Term ∪ C-Wff
- J⟦E⟧s = {(d1, ..., di) ∈ Dsj1x ... xDsji/I⟦W[d1/v1, ..., di/vi]⟧s = true} with E = {(v1, ..., vi)/W}, where W has free variables v1, ..., vi and vi is of sort sji.

Programming Languages Equations

m⟦S1; S2⟧ = m⟦S1⟧ . m⟦S2⟧
m⟦S1 ∪ S2⟧ = m⟦S1⟧ ∪ m⟦S2⟧
m⟦S*⟧ = (m⟦S⟧)*
r m⟦W?⟧ q iff r = q and I⟦W⟧r = True
r m⟦X:=T⟧ q iff q = r[I⟦T⟧r/X]
r m⟦R:=E⟧ q iff q = r[J⟦E⟧r/R]
k⟦proc I(Y1, ..., Ym) = S⟧ = {((c1, ..., cm), (C, B)) ∈
(Dsi1 x ... xDsim) x (UxU)/(C[c1/Y1, ..., cm/Ym], B) ∈ m⟦S⟧}
where Yi is of sort si

6.2 Obtaining a Representation Level Specification – An Example

As we did when passing from level 1 to level 2 of the specification of our example data base application, we pass from level 2 to level 3 by first using a constructive and systematic strategy; at a later stage we shall prove the passage correct.

Obtaining the third level specification means to express in the programming language introduced in the previous section both the kinds of predicates to be used, under the guise of relations, and the query and update functions that will act upon them. The query functions are trivially introduced, by noting that the language allows logical-valued expressions of the form R(t), which yield True if t is in R, and False otherwise.

In order to obtain in a constructive manner procedures that implement the desired update functions, we first correlate the four parts of our structured (semi-formal) description of update functions with the semantics of the statements of the programming language. The parts of the structured description are:

a) intended effects
b) pre-conditions
c) side-effects
d) not-affected elements

In turn, the main statements of the programming language are:

1. assignment
2. test

which can be put together in a procedure body by

3. composition
4. union
5. iteration

From the semantic definitions, one readily sees that, in the simpler cases, an update function f will follow the pattern:

proc f(x) = (pre-conditions?; effects; side-effects) ∪ ~pre-conditions?

or, using the if-then construct:

proc f(x) = if pre-conditions then (effects; side-effects)

The assignment statement is the only way to achieve effects and side-effects, since it alone can modify any values in a state; moreover, all other values in the state are not affected. Relational assignment can be specialized to the insert and delete statements, which handle a single tuple. From the definition of those statements, it is clear that, after inserting a tuple t in a relation R, R(t) is true regardless of the situation at the previous state, and that if t is deleted from R then R(t) is false independently again of the previous state; in both cases nothing else is affected, i.e. except for the value of R(t) the new and the previous states are identical.

We look again at the structured description of the function *cancel*:

τ = *cancel* (c, σ)
intended effects: *offered* (c, τ) = *False*
pre-conditions: $\sim\exists$s (*takes* (s, c, σ) = *True*)
side-effects: none
not-affected: all other queries, including *offered* (c′, .) with c′ $\neq$ c

Using the pattern above, we are led to write:

proc cancel (c) = if $\sim\exists$s TAKES (s, c) then delete OFFERED (c)

More complex updates may require (possibly nested) tests and iterations. The latter are useful, in particular, to check a universally-quantified pre-condition. Explicitly quantified pre-conditions and the general form of assignment lead to a more "set-oriented" style of programming, whereas the use of iteration and insert/delete statements favors a "tuple-oriented" style.

The complete programming language specification for the example is given below:

schema

OFFERED (Courses);
TAKES (Students, Courses);

proc initiate ( )	= (TAKES := Φ; OFFERED := Φ)
proc offer (c)	= insert OFFERED (c)
proc cancel (c)	= if $\sim\exists$s TAKES (s, c) then delete OFFERED (c)
proc enroll (s, c)	= if OFFERED (c) then insert TAKES (s, c)
proc transfer (s, c, c′)	= if TAKES (s, c) $\wedge$ $\sim$TAKES (s, c′) $\wedge$ OFFERED (c′) then (delete TAKES (s, c); insert TAKES (s, c′))

end schema

6.3 Second to Third Level Refinements

We repeat in this section the exercise of Sect. 5.3, this time showing what it means for a representation level specification of a data base application to be a refinement of a functions level specification of the same application.

Let T2 = (L2, A2) and T3 be the functions and representation level specifications of the same data base application. Then, the operations defined by procedures in T3 must satisfy all equations in A2. Again, we must face the fact that T2 and T3 use different formalisms so we do not have a notion of interpretation readily available.

Recall that T3 uses a programming language, which is in turn based on a first-order language, say, L3.

For simplicity, we assume that every parameter sort of L2 is a sort of L3 and every variable of sort s of L2 is also a variable of L3. For simplicity we assume that every parameter sort of L2 is a sort of L3 and every variable of sort s of L2 is also a variable of L3.

The notion of refinement is again formally defined by specifying a mapping K from the non-logical symbols of L2 into non-logical symbols of L3, wffs of L3 and procedure declarations of T3. The mapping K must satisfy the following requirements:

1) for each n-ary update function symbol u of L2 of sort ⟨s1, ..., sn−1, *state*, *state*⟩, K(u) is a procedure declaration proc U(y1, ..., yn−1) = S in T3 such that yi is of sort si, for i = 1, ..., n−1.
2) for each n-ary query function symbol q of L2 of sort ⟨s1, ..., sn−1, *state*, *Boolean*⟩, K(q) is a wff of L3 with free variables x1, ..., xn−1 of sorts s1, ..., sn−1
3) for each n-ary function symbol f of L2 of sort ⟨s1, ..., sn, *Boolean*⟩, except those in 2) and those representing logical connectives, K(f) is a wff of L3 with free variables x1, ..., xn of sorts s1, ..., sn
4) for each n-ary function symbol f of L2 of sort ⟨s1, ..., sn, sn+1⟩, with sn+1 not equal to *Boolean* or *state*, K(f) = f

Note: the requirement in 4) could be generalized to K(f) being a wff of L3 with free variables x1, ..., xn, y of sorts s1, ..., sn+1, if we could force the wff K(f) to define a function as for first-order interpretations.

We now pause for a comment from our formalisms department.

If the reader remembers Sect. 4.3, the next natural step would be to extend K to map wffs of L2 into wffs of L3. However, L3 is not powerful enough to permit us to carry on such extension. In order to do so, we would need a full programming logic, such as Dynamic Logic. To circumvent this difficulty, we adopt a semantic definition of correct refinement.

Thus, using an interpretation K, we define a mapping N from finitely generated universes of L3 into finitely generated structures of L2, defined as follows.

Let U be a finitely generated universe of L3. That is, U is a set of structures of L3 differing only on the relation names declared in T3 and on the scalar program variables of L3 such that U is generated by the procedures declared in T3. We also assume that each procedure p declared in T3 is deterministic. Thus, if p has parameters of sorts s1, ..., sn, then the semantic equations associate with p a function

$$k[\![p]\!]: Ds1 \text{ x} \ldots \text{x } Dsn \text{ x} U \rightarrow U$$

Now, N(U) is a structure A of L2 defined as follows. Let E be any structure of L3 in U:

1) The domain of A of each parameter sort s coincides with the domain of E of sort s (this is well-defined because every parameter sort of L2 is also a sort of L3, by assumption, and two structures in U have the same domains).

The domain of sort *state* is U itself, the domain of sort *Boolean* is {true, false};

2) if u is an n-ary update function symbol of L2, $A(u) = k[\![K(u)]\!]$;
3) if q is an n-ary query function symbol of L2, A(q) is the function defined by K(q), that is,

$$A(q) = \{(a1, \ldots, an-1, E, true)/E \models K(q)\ [a1/x1, \ldots, an-1/xn-1]\} \cup \{(a1, \ldots, an-1, E, false)/E \not\models K(q)\ [a1/x1, \ldots, an-1/xn-1]\}$$

4) if f is an n-ary function symbol of L2 of sort ⟨s1, ..., sn; *Boolean*⟩, except the query function symbols and those representing logical connectives, A(q) is the function defined by K(q), that is,

$$A(q) = \{(a1, \ldots, an, true)/E \models K(q)\ [a1/x1, \ldots, an/xn]\} \cup \{(a1, \ldots, an, false)/E \not\models K(q)\ [a1/x1, \ldots, an/xn]\}$$

5) if f is a function symbol of L2 of sort ⟨s1, ..., sn, sn+1⟩ with sn+1 not equal to *boolean* or *state*, A(f) = E(K(f))
6) if c is a constant of L2, A(c) = E(K(c))
7) if = is the equality symbol of L2 of sort ⟨s, s, *Boolean*⟩,

$$A(=) = \{(a1, a2, true)/E \models a1 = a2\} \cup \{(a1, a2, false)/E \models a1 \neq a2\}$$

8) if f is a function symbol of L2 of sort ⟨*Boolean*, *Boolean*, *Boolean*⟩ or ⟨*Boolean*, *Boolean*⟩ standing for one of the logical connectives, A(f) is a representation of the truth table of the connective

We can prove that, since U is a finitely generated universe of L3, N(U) is a finitely generated structure of L2.

Since it is not possible to map wffs of L2 into wffs of some formal language connected to T3, theorem 4.1 has no counterpart here.

Now, using N, we precisely characterize when T3 is a correct refinement of T2.

Definition – We say that T3 is a correct refinement of T2, under a given interpretation K, iff for every finitely generated universe U of L3, N(A) is a model of T2.

This concludes our discussion about second to third level refinements.

6.4 Proof of Correctness of the Refinement – An Example

On analysing the constructive strategy (Sect. 6.2) we observe that the semi-formal considerations that resulted in the algebraic equations of the second level were used but not the equations themselves. Similarly, our understanding of the semantics of the programming language constructs described denotationally was used but, again, the formal denotational description does not appear directly in the process. Finally, we insisted on writing the specification strictly as imposed by the syntactical description of the language, without however making explicit usage of the grammar productions. The formal machinery is necessary, and thereby justified, when we proceed to the verification of correctness, to be developed in the sequel.

We have to verify that the representation level is a correct refinement of the functions level. This amounts to checking, basically, that the procedures define update functions satisfying the equations of the algebraic specification, once the syntactical correctness of the programming language specification is ascertained.

In order to verify that the above programming language specification is syntactically correct we have to guarantee that it can be generated by the W-grammar in Sect. 6.1.1. Since p is the start symbol, we have to check that the specification is, so to speak, of the form

repr Q, where Q defined

In view of the metarule for Q, this amounts to

(*) repr schema SCL; OPL end-schema,
where schema SCL; OPL end-schema defined

Now, using the metarule for SCL together with the rules inherited from the underlying grammar GL we can generate the following metaproduction of SCL

OFFERED (S), TAKES (S, C)

Similarly, using the metarules for OPL, OP and S together with rules inherited from GL we can generate the following metaproduction of OPL

proc initiate ( ) = ... ;
proc transfer (s, c, c′) =
([TAKES (s, c) ∧ ∼TAKES (s, c′) ∧ OFFERED (c′)]?;
[TAKES := {(y1, y2)/TAKES (y1, y2) ∧ ∼(y1 = s ∧ y2 = c)};
TAKES := {(y1, y2)/TAKES (y1, y2) ∨ (y1 = s ∧ y2 = c′)}]) ∪
(∼[TAKES (s, c) ∧ ∼TAKES (s, c′) ∧ OFFERED (c′)])?

We can now uniformly replace each occurrence of SCL and OPL in (*) by the corresponding metaproduction. Then application of the "repr" programming language hyperrules will convert the "repr" part of (*) into terminals.

It remains to check that the "where" part (a predicate) of (*) reduces to &. This amounts to checking that each wff used in a test, such as TAKES (s, c) ∧ ∼TAKES (s, c′) ∧ OFFERED (c′) is indeed closed and that the lefthand and righthand sides of the assignments have the same types, besides checking that all relational program variables in OPL are indeed declared in SCL.

Thus, the predicate succeeds and we generate a sequence of terminal symbols, which becomes our programming language specification upon application of the definitions of the constructs *if . . . then*, *insert*, etc.

Therefore, we have ascertained the syntactical correctness of our specification.

We now outline how we can verify that the representation level specification T3 (Sect. 6.2) is a correct refinement of the functions level specification T2 = (L2, A2) (Sect. 5.2) under the interpretation K defined below:

K (*offered*) = OFFERED (c)
K (*takes*) = TAKES (s, c)
K (u) = U, where u is an update function and U is the homonym procedure

Let L3 be the underlying language of T3.

Intuitively, given a universe U for T3, the interpretation K induces a finitely generated structure A for L2. At this point, it suffices to clarify that each element p of the domain of the sort *state* of A will be in fact a structure in U. From now on, we will refer to such elements simply as States and use p, q, r, ..., with subscripts if necessary, to denote them (the reader must therefore bear in mind that states are structures of L3).

Moreover, the domain of sort *state* of A is finitely generated by construction. That is, each element p of the domain of sort *state* of A is the value of a term of L2, which is schematically of the form:

un (un − 1 (... u1 (u0) ...))

where u0 is the update function symbol *initiate* of L2 and ui, with i = 1, ..., n, are also update function symbols of L2. Intuitively, since the data base application is encapsulated by the query and update functions, the current data base state can be represented by such terms, indicating the operations used thus far.

To prove that T3 is a correct refinement of T2 amounts to proving that each of the conditional equations in A2 is (universally) valid in A. Now, since A is finitely generated and in view of the previous discussion, we can in fact do an induction on the length of the terms corresponding to each element of the domain States of sort *state* of A. That is, for each P in A2, we will prove by induction on n that P is valid in A when the variable σ receives as value some state which is in turn the value of a term un (un − 1 (... (*initiate*) ...)) of L2.

The basis is trivial. So assume that each P in A2 is valid in A when the state variable σ receives as value some state p and p is the value of a term un − 1 (un − 2 (... (*initiate*) ...)) of L2. We will show that this result holds when we consider terms of length n.

Now, let q be an element of States and assume that q is the value of a term un (un − 1 (... (*initiate*) ...)) of L2.

As an example, consider Eq. 6, namely

1) *offered* (c, *cancel* (c, σ)) = *true* ≡ ∃*s* (*takes* (s, c, σ) = *True*)

This equation is (universally) valid in A when σ is valuated as p iff the following condition holds (from now on, C will denote the domain of sort *course* of A, T will denote the domain of sort *student* of A and S will denote the domain of sort *state* of A), where q is the state that the data base will reach upon application of the procedure to cancel course c at state p:

I ⟦OFFERED (c)⟧ q = I ⟦∃s TAKES (s, c)⟧p, where (p, q) ∈ k ⟦cancel (c′)⟧(c)

Let us consider the procedure for the update cancel. By means of the semantic equations together with the definition of the constructs *if ... then* and *delete*, we obtain, for each s in the domain of S,

$k[\![\text{proc cancel (c)} = \textit{if} \sim\exists s \text{ TAKES (s, c) } \textit{then delete} \text{ OFFERED (c)}]\!](c) =$

$m[\![\textit{if} \sim\exists s \text{ TAKES (s, c) } \textit{then delete} \text{ OFFERED (c)}]\!] =$

$\{(p, q) \in (U\times U)/I[\![\exists s \text{ TAKES (s, c)}]\!]p = \text{False and}$
$q = p[\{x \in C/I[\![\text{OFFERED (x)}]\!]p = \text{True and}$
$I[\![x]\!]p \neq I[\![c]\!]p\}/\text{OFFERED}])\} \cup$
$\{(p, q) \in (U\times U)/I[\![\exists s \text{ TAKES (s, c)}]\!]p = \text{True and } q = p\}$

In view of the form of the expression above giving the meaning of procedure cancel, it is natural to divide this verification into two cases, according to the value of $I[\![\exists s \text{ TAKES (s, c)}]\!]p$.

Case 1: $I[\![\exists s \text{ TAKES (s, c)}]\!]p = \text{False}$

Then $(p, q) \in m[\![\textit{if} \sim\exists s \text{ TAKES (s, c) } \textit{then delete} \text{ OFFERED (c)}]\!]$
iff $q = p[\{x \in C/I[\![\text{OFFERED (x)}]\!]p = \text{True and}$
$I[\![x]\!]p \neq I[\![c]\!]p\}/\text{OFFERED}]$

Thus $I[\![\text{OFFERED (c)}]\!]q = \text{False} = I[\![\exists s \text{ TAKES (s, c)}]\!]p$.

Case 2: $I[\![\exists s \text{ TAKES (s, c)}]\!]p = \text{True}$

Then $(p, q) \in m[\![\textit{if} \sim\exists s \text{ TAKES (s, c) } \textit{then delete} \text{ OFFERED (c)}]\!]$ iff $q = p$

Hence $I[\![\text{OFFERED (c)}]\!]q = I[\![\text{OFFERED (c)}]\!]p$

Let ri be the state denoted by the term ui (ui − 1 (... (*initiate*)...)), for i = 0, ..., n (hence rn − 1 = p and rn = q). By the induction hypothesis, each equation P in A2 is valid in A when σ is valuated as ri and c is valuated as b, for i = 0, ..., n − 1. (We use $A \models P[b/c, ri/\sigma]$ to indicate this condition.)

Let us proceed in a *backward direction* to examine the various possibilities for each ui, for any b′, b″ ∈ C and t, t′ ∈ T:

1) if ui is *initiate* then, by Eq. 2,

$A \models (\textit{takes}\ (s, c, \textit{initiate}) = \textit{False})[t/s, b/c]$

2) if ui is *offer* then, by Eq. 5,

$A \models (\textit{takes}\ (s, c, \textit{offer}\ (c', \sigma)) = \textit{takes}\ (s, c, \sigma))[t/s, b'/c', b/c, ri-1/\sigma]$

3) if ui is *cancel* then, by Eq. 8,

$A \models (\textit{takes}\ (s, c, \textit{cancel}\ (c', \sigma)) = \textit{takes}\ (s, c, \sigma))[t/s, b'/c', b/c, ri-1/\sigma]$

4) if ui is *enroll* then, by Eq. 10

$A \models (\textit{takes}\ (s, c, \textit{enroll}\ (s, c, \sigma)) = \textit{offered}\ (c, \sigma))[t/s, b/c, ri-1/\sigma]$ and by Eq. 11, if $t \neq t'$ and $b \neq b'$:

$A \models (\textit{takes}\ (s, c, \textit{enroll}\ (s', c', \sigma)) =$
$\textit{takes}\ (s, c, \sigma))[t/s, t'/s', b/c, b'/c', ri-1/\sigma]$

5) if ui is *transfer* then, by Eq. 13, 14, 15

$$A \models ((\textit{takes}\ (s, c, \textit{transfer}\ (s', c', c'', \sigma)) = \textit{True} \rightarrow \textit{offered}\ (c, \sigma) = \textit{True} \vee \textit{takes}\ (s, c, \sigma)) = \textit{True})\ [t/s, T'/s', b/c, b'/c', b''/c'', ri-1/\sigma]$$

The backward process uses 1)–5) repeatedly. In many cases we are simply led to examine a previous state, since the expression used says that c is offered after the application of an ui if it was offered at ri – 1. However this process cannot reach *initiate*, where c would not be offered, contrarily to the condition of *case 2*. We can verify that the only way to fulfill this condition, rewritten as

$$A \models (\exists s\ \textit{takes}\ (s, c, \sigma))[b/c, rn-1/\sigma]$$

is either by enrolling s in c or by transferring s to c, in any case in a state ri – 1 where c is offered. Moreover, by Eq. 9 and 12, c will still be offered after any of the two operations is applied. Hence, we conclude that

6) there exists $j < n$ such that

$$A \models (\exists s (\textit{takes}\ (s, c, \sigma) = \textit{True})[b/c, rj/\sigma] \text{ iff}$$
$$A \models (\exists s (\textit{takes}\ (s, c, \sigma) = \textit{True})[b/c, rn-1/\sigma]$$
$$\text{and } A \models (\textit{offered}\ (c, \sigma) = \textit{True})[b/c, rj/\sigma]$$

Let k be the maximum such j. So, we have that

$$A \models (\exists s\ \textit{takes}\ (s, c, \sigma) = \textit{True})[b/c, rk/\sigma] \text{ and}$$
$$A \models (\textit{offered}\ (c, \sigma) = \textit{True})[b/c, rk/\sigma].$$

Now, we can proceed in a *forward direction* to show that indeed

$$A \models (\textit{offered}\ (c, \sigma) = \textit{True})[b/c, rn-1/\sigma].$$

since the only way to reach from rj a state where c is no longer offered is by cancelling c, which fails as long as there is a student taking c (here we are using, among others, Eq. 6, the very equation that we are about to prove; this is legitimate because we are assuming by hypothesis its validity up to state rn – 1).

Hence

$$I [\![\text{OFFERED}(c)]\!]\, q = I [\![\text{OFFERED}(c)]\!]\, p$$

This ends the inductive step for Eq. 6.

Proceeding similarly we can then verify that all the equations of the operations level are satisfied by our specification of the representation level.

Part B
Semantic Data Models

7 Introduction to Part B

In this part of the book we shall investigate data models that are less abstract than those discussed in Part A but which still allow us to express the meaning – semantics – and ultimate purpose of the data and data manipulation activities the application wants to incorporate in the information system. All of them could be thought to belong to the representation level of specifying the conceptual schema of a data base as introduced in the introductory chapter of this book.

For the reason of wanting to be oriented towards the semantic of data and data manipulation, we shall exclude from our consideration the, we could call them original, data models represented by the network, hierarchical and relational approaches. They have been described extensively, see for example [Da], and have not been developed primarily for the representation of the meaning of data, but rather as tools for expressing the structure and organization, i.e. the syntax, of the data. Belatedly, some attempts have been made to add concepts for describing at least some of the meaning of data to these approaches, e.g. E.F. Codd's RM/T model [Co]. These attempts, we believe, tend to confuse the clearly required separation between syntactic structures and semantic properties even further, and we therefore shall concentrate here on data modelling principles that have been developed expressively with the idea of representing the meaning of data and not their logical or physical structure. Unfortunately, the literature does not clearly distinguish between data models for meaning representations and those for data structuring. Even the recent report by ISO TC97/SC5/WG3 [ISO] does nothing to clarify this matter as it classifies modelling techniques not by the very fundamental "meaning" versus "structure" principles but rather according to the relatively minor properties on whether or not values are seen as objects in their own right or whether or not state-oriented/navigational facilities exist in the models.

Even restricting ourselves to semantic data models leaves us with much too large a range of models to be discussed in the present framework. The interested reader is therefore referred to an early comparison [BN1] and to the extensive description and literature references given in [TL]. Modern approaches even include many of the concepts and tools that have been developed for software engineering, where system life cycles, analysis, design specification, and maintainance principles have orginated, but are now applied to the field of information systems. The proceedings of the IFIP TC8 Working Conferences CRIS I [OSV] and CRIS II [OST] contain a number of such approaches. In CRIS I all papers use as an example the same IFIP Working Conference Information System and in [TF] the sometimes neglected problem of physial data base design is discussed extensively.

The first semantic data model to be presented here is the *Logical Database Model* described in [BN2]. It is used mainly to argue what is actually to be included in a semantic data model and how the respective concepts could be described. The second model to be discussed is the Entity Relationship Model originally proposed in [Che 1] and later extended by numerous other authors, many of them represented in the proceedings of three Entity Relationship Conferences that have taken place in 1979, 1981, and 1983 [Che 2, Che 3, DJNY]. These conferences show that the ER-Model is currently probably the most widely used semantic data model in existence. The third model to be described here is of much more recent origin. It tries to incorporate both semantic data modelling and action modelling principles to allow for the full specification of an application oriented information system [Sc 1, Sc 3].

By choosing these three models we do not claim that these models are the best or most complete, but we feel that they represent nicely three of the most widely used approaches to semantic modelling of information systems, by expressing:

Model 1: atomic (unstructured) objects, object classifications and relationships between objects

Model 2: complex objects, properties of objects, object classifications and relationships between objects

Model 3: complex objects, object classification, relationship between objects, actions on objects according to abstract data type principles, time related properties of objects and actions.

Of course, none of these approaches are able to handle information systems which deal with texts, pictures, voice and dimensional descriptions as they appear in text processing, graphics, audiovisual systems and CAD/CAM for example. In fact, very few general results have appeared in these areas and much more research work will be needed until they are as well understood as the "formatted data" handled by the models discussed in this book.

8 The Logical Database Model

The Logical Database Model has been proposed in [BN2] and it is especially careful to give a precise definition of what a semantic data model is to achieve and how such models are to relate to the real world on one hand and to the database implementation on the other.

The representation of the meaning of data is the main purpose of a semantic data model and this meaning is important for a variety of reasons:

1) Different persons designing/extending a database have to have an identical understanding of what the data in the database mean. Wrong/inconsistent definitions may otherwise be produced, destroying the correctness of the information kept in the database.
2) Mappings into the internal database representation will only be made correctly and consistently if the properties of the data to be represented are clearly understood. Value ranges and dependencies between data items may otherwise be designed incorrectly.
3) Different users may see only (overlapping) parts of the whole database. These views, however, have all to be mapped to the same conceptual database description and ultimately database data. The consistency of these views can only be checked by using the concept of data equivalence which again has to be based on the semantic of the data kept in the database.

Let us illustrate this problem of giving an interpretation to data on a very simple example based on the conventional relational data base model.

The information we want to represent concerns divisions of a company and the production oriented activities that are performed in the divisions.

One possible relational structure for these facts is shown in the data base schema of Fig. 8.1a. The schema identifies the data describing the divisions as division number,

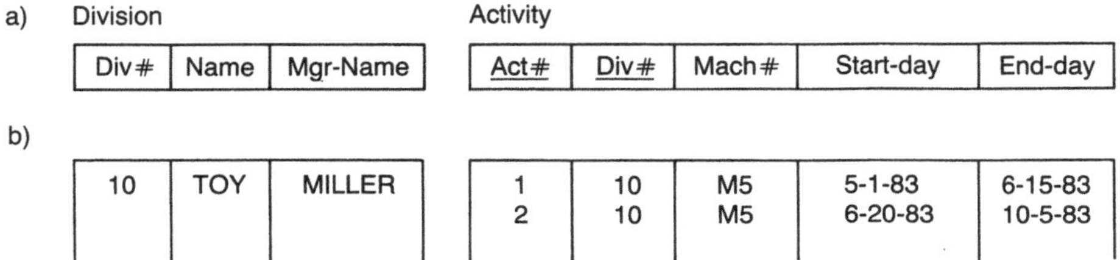

a) Division

Div#	Name	Mgr-Name

Activity

Act#	Div#	Mach#	Start-day	End-day

b)

10	TOY	MILLER

1	10	M5	5-1-83	6-15-83
2	10	M5	6-20-83	10-5-83

Fig. 8.1a, b. A relational data base A

name of the division, and name of its manager. An activity of a division (Div #) is described using an activity number, a machine identification and the start and end days of machine usage for that activity. In Fig. 8.1b one instance of a division together with the instances of the associated activities are presented. A set of facts possibly represented by these instances is:

F_A = {Division n. 10 has the name Toy and the manager Miller. Activity no. 1 of division no. 10 needs the machine M5 from 5-1-83 to 6-15-83. Activity no. 2 of division no. 10 needs the machine M5 from 6-20-83 to 10-5-83.}

Another possible representation of the divisional activities in a relational data base is shown in Fig. 8.2. In Fig. 8.2a the schema identifies only a single relation containing all the data

a) Division Activities

Div#	Act#	Name	Mgr-Name	Mach#	Start-day	End-day

b)

10	1	TOY	MILLER	M5	5-1-83	6-15-83
10	2	TOY	MILLER	M5	6-20-83	10-5-83

Fig. 8.2a, b. A relational data base B

describing divisions and associated activities. In Fig. 8.2b two instances of the relation are shown. They could represent the set of facts

F_{B^1} = {The division activity with division no. 10 and activity no. 1 has the name TOY, the manager MILLER, and uses machine no. M5 from 5-1-83 to 6-15-83. The division activity with division no. 10 and activity no. 2 has the name TOY, the manager MILLER, and uses machine no. M5 from 6-20-83 to 10-5-83}.

To prove that the sets F_A und F_{B^1} represent the same information is certainly not easy. Actually F_{B^1} conveys the quite different information that activities, not divisions, have names and managers associated which would not be an obvious conclusion drawn from the facts in F_A. If we, however, interpret Fig. 8.2b to represent the facts

F_{B^2} = {The division no. 10 has the name TOY and the manager MILLER and the activity no. 1 of division no. 10 needs machine no. M5 from 5-1-83 to 6-15-83. The division no. 10 has the name TOY and the manager MILLER and the activity no. 2 of division no. 10 needs machine no. M5 from 6-20-83 to 10-5-83}.

then the equivalence between F_A and F_{B^2} can easily be shown as the first sentence in F_{B^2} is the conjunction of the sentences 1 and 2 in F_A and the second sentence in F_{B^2} is the conjunction of the sentences 1 and 3 in F_A.

From this example it should be clear that the simple data representation information contained in a relational data base is not sufficient to guarantee a unique interpretation by the different users of the data base. Additional information has to be given which concerns the *information content* of the data before we can assume that every user will interpret the data in a data base identically. In the next section we shall introduce a model that will help us to determine the kind of structures and mechanisms required for representing information in data base systems.

8.1 The Semantic Framework

In this section we introduce the precise definition of what we understand when we speak of the semantics of data bases. In Fig. 8.3 we present the situation in which we find ourselves as data base users at a specific time t.

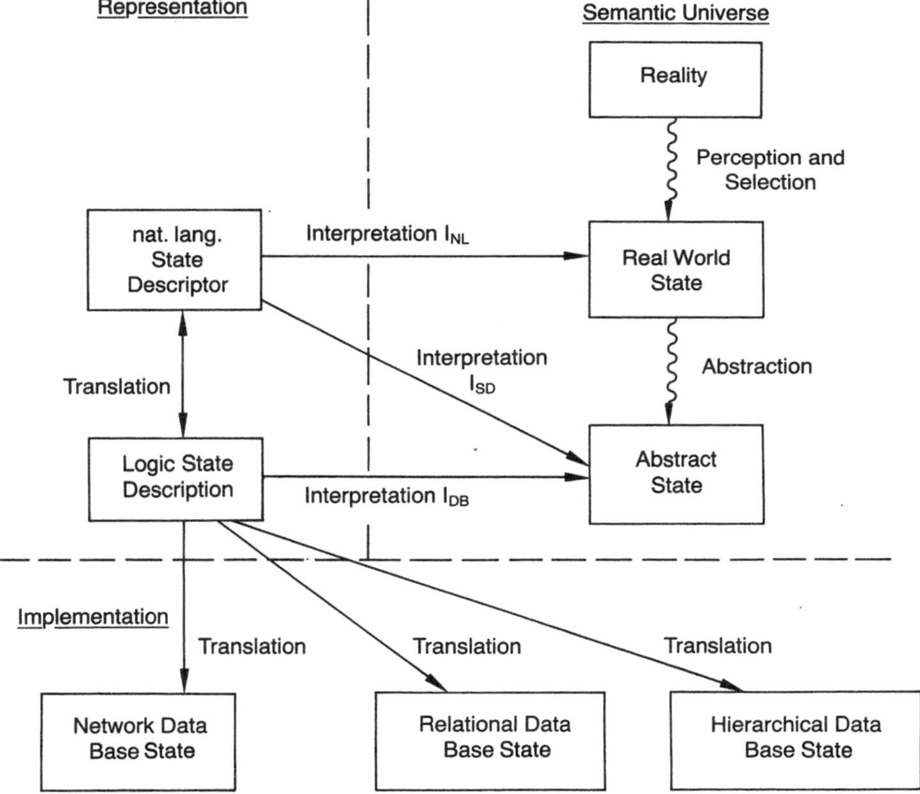

Fig. 8.3 The data base world at a time t

8.1.1 Reality and the Real World States

At any time t only part of all the facts that could be stated about *reality* are of interest to the data base system. It is, however, essential that all the users agree which part of the facts is relevant and which is not, as this will determine the contents of the data base at time t. In other words, a perception and selection process is applied to reality to extract at time t a slice – the *real world state* – which we intend to represent in the data base. Of course, at each moment of time a different real world state may have to be represented and we shall speak about the *universe of discourse* as the union of all real world states that may exist at some point of time. The universe of discourse here simply is formed by the set of all imaginable real world states. Notice that with this definition we have excluded from our discussion the operations and activities that may be performed using the data base. In Chap. 10 we shall extend our discussion to include activities performed but for the moment we shall concentrate on data and information contained in the data base.

The fundamental concepts of the real world state are *objects* which possess *properties* and between which *relationships* may exist.

An *object* is anything about which facts can be reported i.e. something that can appear in the subject or object position of an English sentence. Objects can be concrete (the book that you are currently reading) or abstract (the integer value 2975), they may be simple (the color red) or complex (the set of all parts stored in a specific warehouse).

A property is denoted as a predicative expression in natural language (to be an employee, to be red). A property can be the conjunction or the disjunction of other properties. For example the property "to be husband" is the conjunction of the properties "to be male" and "to be married". "To be employee" could be the disjunction of "to be secretary", "to be engineer", "to be manager", etc.

A relationship is denoted by natural language verbs that connect objects together as for example "is married to" or "is employed by".

Unfortunately, these concepts cannot be defined formally and consequently it is possible that the perception and selection process as applied by different persons on the same part of reality will result in different real world states. We shall call these different real world states *conceptually different views.* For example one view may regard colors to be properties of objects, e.g. "to be red", "to be green", whereas another introduces colors as objects, e.g. "red", "green" and represent colors of objects by a relationship "has color". However there exists an essential difference between these two views. In the second case further facts about colors can be represented, e.g. "the wave length of the color red is between 0,65 and 0,75 Angström". This is not possible when colors are not represented as objects.

Another consequence of being unable to define the concepts object, property, relationship, and the perception process formally is, that we are unable to prove that two real world states are describing the same slice of reality or that the universe of discourse we have selected actually comprises the slice of reality that we originally intended to incorporate into our data base system.

8.1.2 The Natural Language State Description

A real world state is completely determined if it is known which objects exist, which properties they possess, and which relationships between them exist. In other words, a real world state is determined if one knows all the facts that are correct at that specific point of time.

To describe these facts, we normally use predicative English sentences. This description is called a *state description*. Since we have presupposed that all users agree on facts to be relevant or not, it is sufficient to represent at time t a real world state by only those sentences that are true at that time. Then all the facts that are relevant but not included in the state description are false.

An *elementary sentence* of the state description in general contains three components, a subject-, a predicate- and an object-part consisting of none, one, or more denotations of objects. We assume that an elementary sentence cannot be split into a conjunction of other elementary sentences that conveys the same information about facts. Examples of elementary sentences are:

"Bill Smith is an employee."
"Division no. 1 has the manager John."
"Activity no. 1 of division no. 10 needs machine no. M 5".

The subject- and object-part denotations need not be simple, they can also be structured as in the third example above.

Whether a sentence is elementary or not can only be decided with respect to a certain universe of discourse. In the above example we have assumed that activities have unique numbers within divisions, but if we should decide that our universe of discourse actually deals with activity numbers unique throughout all divisions, the above sentence could be restructured as

"Activity no. 1 is in division no. 10 *and*
Activity no. 1 needs machine no. M 5."

The original information is now conveyed by a conjunction of two sentences and the original sentence is not elementary any more.

Since we assumed that all users of the data base agree on the universe of discourse, we can now assume that all the users would agree at any point of time that a given state description is true – i.e. represents all the facts that are true with respect to the real world state at that time – or that it is false. This means that all users understand a common language (i.e. English) and that we use that language as our *representation* language for the real world states. The *natural language interpretation* I_{NL} of a state description then can be understood to map the phrases in the sentences to the objects, properties and relationships of the real world state.

8.1.3 The Abstract Model and the Standard Interpretation

The universe of discourse is a conceptualization of the reality as it actually exists but it does not lend itself to formal treatment. To be able to formalize the semantics –

i.e. the meaning – of data bases we need a formally defined universe of discourse. To achieve this goal, we introduce an *abstract* (*world*) *model* as a set of *abstract states*.

An abstract state is a mathematical construct – an abstract data structure if you will – consisting of a set E of *entities*, a family T of *types*, and a family R of *relations*. In addition, every type T_i which is an element of T is a subset of the set E, and the union of all the types in T is the set E. With any relation R_i which is an element of R a rank n_i is associated and R_i is a subset of E^{ni}.

In an abstract (world) model every abstract state must contain the same number of types and the same number of relations whereby it is possible that a type or relation may be empty.

To discuss the interrelationship between a real world state and an abstract state we are going to use the state description and the *standard interpretation* I_{SD}.

A standard interpretation is a mapping which assigns entities to noun phrases, types and relations to verb phrases and the values *true* or *false* to sentences. A verb phrase is mapped to a type if it denotes a property, and to a relation if it denotes a relationship. A standard interpretation maps in all state descriptions the same noun phrase to the same entity and the same verb phrase to the same type respectively relation.

A sentence of a state description either states that an object possesses a property or that a relationship exists between some objects. In the first case the sentence is mapped to the value *true* if the entity to which the noun phrase of the sentence is mapped is an element of the type identified by the verb phrase, otherwise it is mapped to the value *false*. In the second case the entities to which the subject and object parts of the sentence are mapped form a tuple $\langle e_1, \ldots e_n \rangle$. The sentence is mapped to the value *true*, if this tuple is an element of the relation identified by the verb phrase, otherwise it is mapped to the value *false*.

An abstract state is called a *model* of a state description, if a standard interpretation exists such that all sentences of the state description are mapped to the value *true* and all sentences not part of the state description are mapped to the value *false*.

Let SD be a state description, RW the associated real world state, and AS an abstract state which is a model of SD. Then AS is called an *abstraction* of the real world state RW. An entity e is called an abstraction of an object o, if a noun phrase denoting o in SD is mapped to the entity e. The type T_p is called the abstraction of the property p, if the verb phrase denoting p in SD is mapped to the type T_p and the abstraction e of the object that possesses that property is an element of T_p. A relation R_r is called an abstraction of relationship r if the verb phrase denoting r is mapped to the relation R_r and the tuple formed by the abstraction of the objects having that relationship r is an element of R_r.

The *abstract model* or *abstract universe of discourse* is an abstraction of the universe of discourse if it is the set of all abstract states which are models of the state descriptions that are true with respect to the universe of discourse.

8.1.4 The Logical State Description and the Interpretation I_{DB}

An abstract state is an abstraction of real world facts and we have used it as the range of the interpretation I_{SD} of the natural language state description. That is, the state description can be considered to provide a representation of the abstract state and we can use this representation whenever we want to talk about the components of the abstract state. For several reasons this representation is not very useful as can be seen in the state description given in Fig. 8.4 where we have reflected the objects, properties and relationships contained in our example of Fig. 8.1.

a) To identify objects unambiguously it is sometimes necessary to use quite cumbersome names, e.g. "the activity with the activity number 1 of the division with division number 10".
b) The use of elementary sentences in the state description forces us to be very repetitive.
c) Nothing guarantees that we always use the same name for the same object. To construct a standard interpretation I_{SD} then becomes a very complicated task. We could, for example, identify our division sometimes by
   "division with division no. 10."
   or sometimes by
   "division with the manager with name MILLER."
   and we would have to detect that these phrases describe the same object.

```
SD = {"Division with division no. 10 has division no. 10.
      Division with division no. 10 has name TOY.
      Division with division no. 10 has manager with name MILLER.
      Manager with name MILLER has name MILLER.
      Division with division no. 10 has activity with
        activity no. 1 of division with division no. 10.
      Division with division no. 10 has activity with
        activity no. 2 of division with division no. 10.
      Activity with activity no. 1 of division with
        division no. 10 has activity number 1.
      ..."}
```

Fig. 8.4. A (partial) natural language state description

In Fig. 8.5 the (partial) abstract state is given which corresponds to the natural language state description of Fig. 8.4 when using a standard interpretation I_{SD}. To be able to represent the abstract state we have used the noun and verb phrases of the state description.

In addition to the problem discussed above we are also faced with the problem to decide whether a natural language phrase *for all times* will be able to identify a specific object, property or relation. For example, to identify a division by its number or by its manager in our description of the abstract state at time t does not automatically ensure that the same identification is possible at time $t + 1$. Only if we know that at all times divisions are numbered uniquely and that a manager always can head only one division becomes our state description a "stable" one in the sense that we do not have to change the identifications of objects, properties and relations every time a change in the real world state is to be reflected.

```
E =  {"division with division no. 10", "division no. 10",
      "TOY", "manager with name MILLER", "MILLER",
       ...}
T =  {"is division" = {"division with division no. 10"},
      "is number of division" = {"division no. 10"},
      "is division name" = {"TOY"},
      "is manager" = {"manager with name MILLER"},
       ...}
R =  {"division has div. no." = { ("division with division no. 10",
                                              "division no. 10")},
      "division has name" = {("division with division no. 10",
                                                       „TOY")},
      "division has manager" = {("division with division no. 10",
                                   "manager with name MILLER")},
       ...},
```

Fig. 8.5. A (partial) abstract state

To solve the problem of a precise and compact description of an abstract state we introduce the *logical state description.* The logical state description is expressed in an artificial language, the *logical data language* (LDL) designed specifically for the purpose of representing entities, types and relations. The structure of LDL sentences is similar to the structure of the elementary predicative sentences of a state description and it is described in more detail in Sect. 8.3. The semantics of a logical state description are given by the *database interpretation* I_{DB}, a mapping assigning entities to entity names, relations to relation names and types to type names, and the values *true* or *false* to LDL sentences.

We can now formally define the *correctness* of a logical state description.

A logical state description LSD is correct with respect to an abstract state if an interpretation I_{DB} exists such that all sentences of LSD are mapped to the value *true* and all LDL sentences which are not contained in L_{SD} are mapped to the value *false* using mapping rules analogous to those explained for I_{SD} before. That is, a sentence identifying the type of an entity will be true if the entity is a member of that type in the abstract state. A sentence identifying a relation between entities will be true if the corresponding entity tuple is an element of that relation in the abstract state.

The interrelationship between logical state descriptions and a natural language state description is given by a translation from LDL sentences into natural language sentences. Note that this translation works in two directions in the sense that we shall choose entity names, type names and relation names to closely reflect the names used in the natural language state description for the corresponding objects, properties and relationships. The translation of LDL sentences into natural language sentences is straight forward under these conditions and can be used to tie "real world meaning" to LDL sentences.

To solve the problem of stability of denotations mentioned above but also to be able to talk about the set of all possible abstract states in the abstract model i.e. the abstract universe of discourse, we introduce a second language – the *logical data definition language* (LDDL – see Sect. 8.8). This language can be used to specify the *logical schema* whereby the semantics of the schema are determined by a mapping from the schema to the abstract model. It now becomes possible to state the behaviour that abstract states have to have "at all times" and thereby reflect the behaviour of the real world in areas which cannot directly be represented by objects, properties of objects and relationships between objects. In the logical schema we can now identify whether a manager must "at all times" manage precisely one division. Looking at a single abstract or real world state does not allow us to answer such questions. The logical schema would even allow us to state what possible state transitions between the different real world states are possible, thereby specifying the acivities that take place in the universe of discourse and consequently must be reflected in the abstract model. We shall wait, however, until Chap. 10 before we discuss these aspects of modelling the semantics of data bases.

Notice that the logical schema of the abstract data base would loosely correspond to the schema of the conventional data bases (see Fig. 8.1 a) whereas the logical state description corresponds to the representation of a specific conventional data base instance as shown in Fig. 8.1 b. The principal difference arises from the fact that the logical state description and the logical schema is derived from the real world and directly reflects the meaning of the real world objects, properties and relationships whereas any formal connection to the real world is missing in schemas and representations of conventional data bases.

8.1.5 Conventional Data Bases – The Syntactical View

A logical state description is a formal representation of facts and it can be used for the interpretation and translation of conventional relational network, or hierarchical data base states.

A *conventional data base state* is a set of *data instances* each of which can be regarded to be a representation of one or several facts. The set of all possible, i.e. *syntactically*, correct states is determined by specifying a *data base schema*, i.e. a set of sentences of a *data definition language*, together with rules, how data instances can be derived from schema components. The set of all such syntactically defined data base states should now correspond precisely to the set of abstract states allowed in the abstract model.

The meaning, i.e. the semantics, of data base state or a data base schema cannot be directly extracted, instead it has to be given by a mapping of a data base state to a logical state description and therefore an abstract state and of a data base schema to the logical schema and consequently the abstract model.

Using this mapping we can now formally investigate whether a given data base state or schema corresponds to an abstract state respectively abstract model at all, or whether it reflects some other universe of discourse. In addition, we can determine whether two states of the same or of different data base schemas are equivalent in the sense that they reflect the same abstract state. We can also decide whether two different schemas of the same or of different conventional data base models are equivalent in the sense that they reflect the same abstract model.

This mapping can also ensure that all users of a data base will interpret the different data instances and schema components identically and therefore arrive at a common understanding of what facts are represented in the data base. It is important to realize that by this mapping we cannot ensure a common universe of discourse since there is no formal way to compare this understanding with the real world model or test it for contradictions or omissions. However, on the level of the abstract model and the abstract states such a common understanding can be enforced and since a natural language state description for these states can be derived a common understanding of the natural language will ensure a natural language representation of that "abstract" understanding.

8.2 The Logical Data Definition Language

The logical data definition language is a formal language, the sentences of which are called *(logical) schema entities*, and a set of schema entities is called a *(logical)* schema. The logical schema of a data base system has a twofold purpose:

1) It is a representation of the abstract model, i.e. the abstract universe of discourse.
2) It specifies how the different components of the abstract state, i.e. the entities, relations and types, are to be represented in the logical data lanuage.

Since we cannot represent the abstract model by the set of representations of all imaginable abstract states, an axiomatic approach is used. In this approach (see also [Fl]) the abstract model is represented by introducing type names and relation names and by the specification of axioms which must hold for any abstract state which is an element of the abstract model. These axioms are called *consistency conditions* since they restrict the set of abstract world states to states which are abstractions of imaginable real world states, i.e to states consistent with respect to the user's views of the reality. By consistency conditions, the user's knowledge of interdependencies between different components of the imaginable real world states is expressed. For example, if an object has the property to be married, it cannot at the same time be single. This is expressed by the consistency condition, that at any point of time the types "is married" and "is single" must be disjoint.

Consistency conditions of this kind are called *static* consistency conditions in contrast to *dynamic consistency conditions.* By dynamic conditions, dependencies between states and other (successor) states are expressed. Here we shall only discuss static consistency conditions but in Chap. 10 dynamic consistency conditions will be investigated.

Interdependencies of various state components can only be determined through an investigation of the reality. Therefore formal criteria for their existence and about the ways to produce them cannot be given. It will also be impossible to prove that a given set of axioms is complete or that it describes only those abstract states which are abstractions of imaginable real world states.

We shall formulate the conditions in terms of the abstract model, i.e. entities, types, and relations, In conventional data models consistency conditions are frequently contained implicitly in the data structure convention of the model. For example in our relational schema of Fig. 8.1a the condition is implicitly included that a division must have at least zero and at most one name. Other conditions, as for example that a division must have a unique name, are neither explicitly nor implicitly expressed. Additional information, usually based on the syntactical properties of conventional data models, must be given, e.g. via Normal Form Theory [Da]. Since the semantic connection to the real world states is missing, these specifications have remained of doubtful usability.

When developing LDDL, three goals were to be met:

1) The meaning of schema entries with respect to the abstract model should be easily understood. As a consequence, a translation into the terminology of objects, properties and relationships of the real world model should become simple.
2) The consistency conditions for types and relations should be integrated into the schema components describing types and relations of the abstract world.
3) Redundancy is to be avoided, but not at all cost, as redundancy sometimes is useful in checking for definition errors.

A complete specification of the syntax and semantics of LDDL can be found in Biller [Bi]. We shall only discuss it here through the use of some examples.

8.2.1 Type Declarations

A type is a set of entities which is assigned to a property name by the standard interpretation I_{SD}. Depending on the property to be modelled we can distinguish between different type definitions. In Fig. 8.6 the relationship between the different cases is illustrated.

The type declaration part of the schema consists of a list of type declarations each with the general form

⟨type definition⟩ [⟨characteristics⟩] [⟨identification⟩]

where the square brackets [ ] indicate optional clauses.

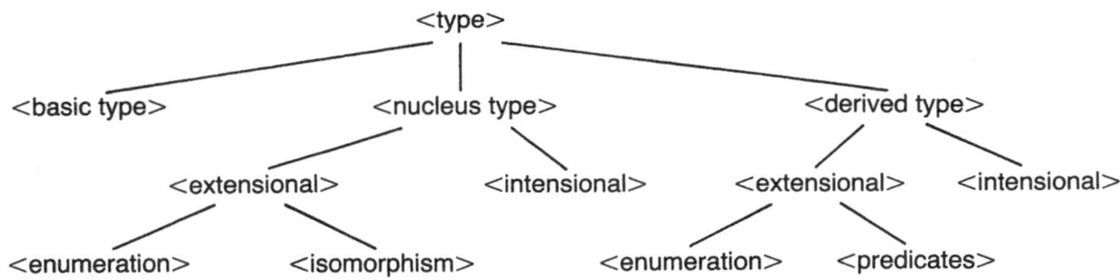

Fig. 8.6. The type classes in LDDL

8.2.2 The ⟨Type Definition⟩ Clause of a Type Declaration

For the *basic types* it is assumed that all users agree upon their meaning so that no consistency rules need to be defined for these types. The representation of these types is used as the starting point for the representation of the other entities in the logical data language. In the data language the entities of these types are represented as constants. To each of the basic types belongs a set of operations, e.g. the arithmetic operations, the relational operations, etc. to the type "is integer", the meaning of which is also assumed to be known to all users. In the following we assume the basic types INTEGER, REAL, STRING, CHARACTER, DIGIT, LETTER, SIGN together with the usual ordering relations and operations.

The format of the definition of a basic type is given by

basic ⟨type name⟩ [*relations* ⟨relational operations⟩]
[*functions* ⟨functional operations⟩]

which for the case of INTEGER may look like

basic INTEGER *relations* $<, \geqq, =, \leqq, <, \neg=$
functions $+, -, *, \div$.

or for STRING

basic STRING *relations* $<, =, >$
functions length, concatenate

For basic types no further specifications are necessary as their meaning is assumed to be understood. Consequently, the declaration parts ⟨characteristics⟩ and ⟨identification⟩ will be empty. For all other types these parts will have the same possible configurations, and they will therefore be introduced after describing the different ⟨type definitions⟩ first.

The *nucleus types* are used to avoid redundancies in the schema and to reduce the number of representations of components of the abstract states to a minimum. The set of nucleus types of an abstract model is defined by (T is the set of types, BT the set of basic types and NT the set of nucleus types):

1) In all abstract states of the abstract model holds
$$\left(\bigcup_{bt \in BT} bt\right) \cap \left(\bigcup_{nt \in NT} nt\right) = \phi$$
2) In all abstract states of the abstract model holds
$$\bigcup_{t \in BT \cup NT} t = \bigcup_{t \in T} t$$
3) There do not exist two different nucleus types T_1 and T_2 such that for all abstract states T_1 is a subset of T_2.

These conditions assure that all types which are neither basic types nor nucleus types can be derived from these types. Therefore a representation for all entities of all abstract states exists if a representation for the basic types and the nucleus types is given.

Since the conditions must hold in all abstract states, we cannot derive the nucleus types formally but only informally from the understanding of the universe of discourse (the real world model).

Nucleus types may be defined either intensionally or extensionally.

The intensional definition of a nucleus type has the form e.g.

type PERSON
type DIVISION

where the ⟨characteristics⟩ and ⟨identification⟩ clauses of these types will add additional information.

The extensional definition of a nucleus type may be given either by an enumeration or by an isomorphism to a basic type.

The enumeration has the form, e.g.

type MONTH *elements* january, february, march, april, may, june, july, august, september, october, november, december

Here the elements are specified by a list of entity representations each identifying one entity of the nucleus type.

A definition using an isomorphism between the nucleus type and the underlying basic type may have many variants, three illustrative examples of which are given in the following.

The nucleus type FIRST NAME is defined by

type FIRST NAME *isomorphic* to STRING
functions length

which specifies that a first name may be any element of the basic type STRING and that (by default) all the relational operations defined for STRING's will be applicable to elements of FIRST NAME. Of the functions, the concatenate operation is not meaningful for first names and is therefore excluded through the above definition.

The nucleus type COUNTRY NAME is defined by

type COUNTRY NAME *isomorphic to* STRING
where length (x) $\leqq 20$
functions nil

and specifies that a country name is a string of length not greater than 20. Free variables (x) are considered to belong to the basic type and to be bound by an universal quantifier.

For the nucleus type SALARY the type definition

type SALARY *isomorphic to* REAL
where $100 * x \in$ INTEGER
relations ($<$, less than), ($>$, greater than)
functions ($+$, $+$) ($-$, $-$),
$*$: SALARY $\times$ REAL $\rightarrow$ SALARY

renames the comparison operations for SALARY values. Addition and subtraction are defined as for REAL numbers, whereas a special multiply operation is introduced, defined between salaries and real numbers and producing a SALARY result value.

Derived types are either intensionally or extensionally defined. An intensionally defined type LEGAL UNIT could be specified by a ⟨type definition⟩ clause of the form

type LEGAL UNIT *subset of* (PERSON $\cup$ COMPANY)

where it is assumed that persons exist which do not have the status of legal units (e.g. children). The intensional definition

type MEMBER OF PARLIAMENT *subset of* PERSON
    where (ιy)(IS AGE OF (y, x)) $\geqq$ AGE (25)

specifies that members of parliament must be persons which are at least 25 years old. (The ι (iota) operator denotes the designation operator of predicate logic).

Extensionally defined derived types can be specified using enumerations or a predicate. In the first case, we can use a ⟨type definition⟩ clause of the form

type SUMMER MONTH *elements* June, July, August of MONTH

to select the three summer months from the type MONTH. Using general predicates, derived type definitions may be specified like

type OF AGE *equal to* PERSON *where*
    (ιy)(IS AGE OF (y, x)) $\geqq$ AGE (18)
type EVEN NUMBERS *equal to* INTEGER
    where $(\exists y)(x = 2 * y)$
type MALE EMPLOYEE *equal to* EMPLOYEE $\cap$ MALE.

8.2.3 The ⟨Characteristics⟩ Clause of a Type Declaration

The *⟨characteristics⟩ clause* of a type declaration is an optional clause as it does not have to exist in every type declaration. It is based on the definition of *characteristic types* and *relations.*

A type T_i is called *characteristic* of a type T_j in an abstract model, if in all abstract states which are elements of the abstract model all elements of the type T_j are also elements of the type T_i. That is, the type T_j is a subset of the type T_i. For example, the type "is person" is characteristic of the type "is employee".

A relation r_i is called *characteristic* of a type T_j *in role k* in an abstract model, if in all abstract states which are elements of the abstract model, the type T_j is a subset of the projection of the relation R_i on the k'th domain. For example, the relation "person has birthday" is characteristic of the type "is person" in role 1, but it is also characteristic of the type "is employee" in role 1.

The existence of a characteristic relation of a type means that a dependency between elements of this type and other entities exists which is called *existence dependency*. If for example a binary relation R is characteristic of a type T in role 1, then the existence of an entity e which is an element of T implies, that an entity e′ (possibly *nil*) exists such that the pair (e, e′) is an element of R.

Characteristic clauses are constructed using type names and relation name role number pairs together with logical operators ∨ (or), + (exclusive or), ¬ (not). The example

characteristics MALE + FEMALE, HAS SOCIAL SEC#.1, HAS NAME.1, HAS BIRTHDAY.1, HAS ADDRESS.1

describes the characteristic types and relations of the type PERSON.

The <characteristics> clause

characteristics MARRIED TO.1

could define the characteristic relation MARRIED TO of the type HUSBAND. HUSBAND however is defined to be a subset of the type PERSON and as a consequence all characteristic types and relations of the type PERSON are also characteristic for HUSBAND (inheritance rule) without being explicitly stated in the characteristics clause of the type declaration for HUSBAND.

The <characteristics> clause

characteristics HAS VALUE IN CURRENCY.1

of type salary specifies the ternary relation between salaries, real numbers and currency designations (i.e. $, DM, FF, ...). This relation defines for every salary entity a relationship to a numeric value together with a currency identification.

8.2.4 The <Identification> Clause of a Type Declaration

In the <identification> clause the *identifying set* of a type is specified. The identifying set of a type is defined as all the types and relations which can be used to uniquely describe the individual entities of the type in all the abstract states contained in an abstract model. Formally the identifying set of a type T is defined as

$$IS = \{T_1, \ldots, T_n, (R_1, i_1), \ldots, (R_m, i_m)\}$$

where the following conditions are satisfied:

1) In all abstract states of an abstract model holds: Let e_1 be an element of T and e_2 be an element of any type in the abstract model, then at least one of the conditions (i) and (ii) must be satisfied:
   (i) A type $T_j \in IS$ exists such that e_1 is an element of T_j and e_2 is not an element of T_j.
   (ii) A pair $(R_j, i_j) \in IS$ and a tuple $r \in R_j$ exists such that $r.i_j = e_1$ and no tuple $r' \in R_j$ exists such that the only difference between r and r′ is that $r'.i_j = e_2$.
2) The set IS is minimal, i.e. if one of the types $T_1, \ldots, T_n$ or one of the relations $R_1, \ldots, R_m$ is taken away the condition 1) is no more satisfied.

Examples of identifying sets are:

Type	IS
"is division"	{("division has no", 1)}
"is division"	{("division has name", 1)}
"is employee"	{"is person", ("has name", 1), ("has address", 1)}

The third example states that an employee may be identified by a name and an address but in addition has to have the property "to be a person" in order to distinguish him from a company which he may have created with his own name and with his own address.

The concept of identifying sets loosely corresponds to the concept of candidate keys in the relational model. But in contrast to candidate keys the definition of identifying set is not based on any representation, but on concepts directly derived from an understanding of the universe of discourse. It is also not required that the relations in an identifying set are functions. For example, if we assume that a person may have several first names and one family name and furthermore that it is impossible that two persons exist with exactly the same set of first and family names, then the identifying set of "is person" is given by the set

{("has first name", 1), ("has family name", 2)}.

The identifying set of a type can be used to represent the entities in the logical data language. The representation of elements is reduced to the representation of the entities which are connected to it by relations contained in the identifying set. For this process to end it is necessary that the elements of some types are represented by constants of the data languages. For basic types and therefore any types isomorphic to a (subset of a) basic type a representation of the elements is presupposed. Any type defined explicitly will, through this declaration, receive a representation for its elements. These types then form the basis for all other entity representations in the logical data language.

The ⟨identification⟩ clause lists the identifying set of a type. Examples are for the types "divisions" and "employees" used above:

identified by {HAS DIVISION NO.}, {HAS NAME}
identified by {IS PERSON, HAS NAME, HAS ADDRESS}

where, if no ambiguities can arise, the role identification number in a relation-number pair can be omitted.

The specification

identified by {*one of* HAS VALUE IN CURRENCY}

is used when more than one tuple in a relation describes the same entity as in our example where a salary s in the relation HAS VALUE IN CURRENCY could be contained in the two tuples

⟨s, 1000, DM⟩
⟨s, 400, $⟩

if we assume an exchange rate of 2.50. Anyone of the pairs (1000, DM), (400, $) will then identify the salary s.

8.2.5 Relation Declarations

By a relation declaration a relation name together with the definition of the domains is introduced. The relation declaration part of the schema consists of a list of such declarations, each with the general form

relation ⟨relation name⟩ [⟨domain definitions⟩]
[⟨consistency constraints⟩]

where square brackets indicate optional clauses.

The two clauses ⟨domain declaration⟩ and ⟨consistency constraints⟩ are concerned with mainly structural characteristics of the relations which can be derived from the real world model since any relation must be an abstraction of a real world relationship.

8.2.6 The ⟨Domain Definitions⟩ Clause of Relation Declarations

Domain definitions restrict a relation to subsets of the cartesian product of certain subsets of the set of entities in the abstract model. The definition for an n-ary relation is given by a list of n domain definitions, whereby for a single domain definition formats can be used that correspond to the formats introduced for the definition of derived types. Examples of domain definitions for the relations DIVISION HAS NAME, HAS TAX ADVISOR, SALARY OF HUSBAND, and IS MARRIED TO are respectively

domains equal to DIVISION, DIVISION NAME
domains (PERSON $\cup$ COMPANY), PERSON
domains SALARY, IS HUSBAND OF .1
domains MALE *where* (ιy)(IS AGE OF $(y, x) \geqq$ AGE(18),
FEMALE *where* (ιy)(IS AGE OF $(y, z) \leqq$ AGE(16).

The first example expresses that all existing DIVISION entities have to appear (in every abstract state) in the projection DIVISION HAS NAME .1, whereas only a subset of the type DIVISION NAME may occur in such relations. The third example uses as the specification of a domain the domain of another relation, expressing the fact that in any abstract state a subset of the entities appearing in the first domain of IS HUSBAND OF may appear in SALARY OF HUSBAND .2. The last example reflects the fact that male persons have to be at least 18 years and female ones at least 16 years before they are allowed to be married.

8.2.7 The ⟨Consistency Constraints⟩ Clause of Relation Declarations

Consistency constraints on the one hand express restrictions that have to hold between domains of a relation but also allow us to specify that a relation may be derived from one or more other relations in the abstract model.

Examples of such restrictions are:

1) *relation* DIVISION HAS ADRESS *restricted by* (1), (2) *min* 1 *max* 3

   which specifies that with a division at least one and at most three addresses can be associated. The general form of a *cardinality restriction* is

   restricted by (integer list), (integer list)
   min integer *max* integer

   and it is defined for a relation R, integer lists L_1 and L_2, and integers i_{min}, i_{max} by the condition

   $(\forall r' \in R.L_1)(i_{min} \leqq |\{r: r \in R.(L_1\, L_2) \wedge r.L_1 = r'\}| \leqq i_{max})$

2) *relation* DIV HAS NAME *funct dep on* (1), (2)

   where the functional dependencies are defined as a special case of cardinality restrictions where L_2 lists all those domains not occurring in L_1 and $i_{min} = i_{max} = 1$. This definition is analogous to the well-known one of the relational data model but since we are dealing here only with irreducible relations, any functional dependency must be between a list of domains and *all* the other domains. In the definition it is therefore only necessary to specify the domain list L_1 since L_2 then always can be identified automatically. In our example, the tuples in the relation DIV HAS NAME are functionally dependent on the domain DIVISION and functionally dependent on the domain DIVISION NAME.

3) *relation* IS GRANDFATHER OF *product of* IS FATHER OF, HAS CHILD

   specifies the equi-join (in relational terminology) of two relations on the last respectively first domain.

4) *relation* HAS NAME *union of* DIV HAS NAME, PERSON HAS NAME

   represents the union of the two relations DIV HAS NAME and PERSON HAS NAME.

This finishes the discussion of the type and relation declarations. A more detailed description and a precise definition of the syntactic and semantic aspests of the introduced concepts can be found in [Bi] and in [BN2].

LDDL contains, besides the declaration of types and relations additional consistency conditions that cannot easily be attached to a single type or relation declaration. In general, these constraints must be expressed by predicate calculus constructs which shall not be further discussed here.

For LDDL no graphical representation has been developed. It was felt that the preciseness of the concepts introduced would lead either to quite complex graphical representations, or the graphical representations would only produce an inprecise picture of the properties of the abstract model as expressed through a logical schema defined by LDDL. In Chap. 9 and 10 of this book semantic modelling techniques are introduced which provide a graphical representation and the techniques employed there could also be utilized to develop a graphical representation for logical schemas specified in the Logical Database Model.

8.3 The Logical Data Language LDL

The logical data language is used to represent the individual states of the abstract model. LDL is a formal language the grammar of which is derived from the schema description philosophy disscussed in the preceding section. Again we shall only discuss the principal features of the language, a complete description is found in [Bi].

Sentences of LDL are either *property instances* or *relation instances*. A property instance specifies that an entity is an element of a type and therefore that the corresponding object of the real world state possesses the property expressed by the type. A relation instance specifies that a tuple of entities is an element of a relation and therefore that for the corresponding objects the relationship holds of which the relation is an abstraction. A *logical data base state* now is the representation of an abstract state and it consists of a set of property instances and relation instances.

To denote property and relation instances it is necessary to introduce a representation, called *entity instances*, for the entities of the abstract model.

To avoid redundancies and interpretation problems every entity should only be represented by exactly one entity instance. Different representation strategies are used depending on whether an entity belongs to a basic type, a nucleus type or a derived type.

The entities of basic types are represented by constants e.g.

−1536, 0, 99, 54400	for integers,
HOUSE, ←∗, JACK	for strings,

and it is assumed that these representations are understood by all users of the data base system.

Nucleus types which are isomorphic to basic types and for which an identification clause is not declared are represented by entity instances of the form

⟨type name⟩ (⟨const⟩)

as for example

NAME (WILSON)
STREET (BROADWAY).

For nucleus types that are defined by enumerations a representation is already included in the type definition. For all other nucleus types the identification clause will be used to develop a unique representation of each entity contained in the type. The general form of the representation is

⟨type name⟩ (⟨descriptor list⟩)

where in the descriptor list the names of the types relevant for the entity to be represented and the relation instances of the relevant relations are listed in the same sequence as specified in the identification clause. The entity to be represented is identified in these relation instances by the symbol *. Examples of such representations are

DATE (MONTH OF (8, *), DAY OF (9, *), YEAR OF (1780, *)
PERSON (HAS FIRST NAME {(*, JOHN), (*, ALLEN)}, HAS FAMILY NAME (*, SMITH))

CANDIDATE (HAS FAMILY NAME (*, (WILSON),
(CANDIDATE IN (*, ELECTION (IN YEAR (*, YEAR (1916)))))

where the last example specifies an entity of the type "(presidential election) candidate".

These representations are quite cumbersome and the following rules allow a simplification for the representation of entity instances:

1) The * is omitted.
2) If the identifying set contains only characteristic relations, the relation names are omitted.
3) If a domain of a relation is defined to be a subset of a nucleus type, the type name is omitted in the relation instence.
4) Parentheses around single entity representations are omitted.

Using these simplifications, our examples become

DATE (8, 9, 1780)
PERSON ({JOHN, ALLEN}, SMITH)
CANDIDATE (WILSON, 1916)

With the help of these entity representations, a property instance can be represented in the form

⟨type instance⟩ (⟨entity instance⟩)

as for example

PRESIDENT (CANDIDATE (CLEVELAND, 1892))

or in simplified form

PRESIDENT (CLEVELAND, 1892)

This property instance is a representation of the fact that the person CLEVELAND which was a presidential CANDIDATE in 1892 became one of the presidents of the United States.

The general representation of relation instances is given by

⟨relation name⟩ (⟨instance list⟩)

and examples are

HAS ADDRESS (({JOHN, ALLEN}, SMITH), NEW YORK)
CANDIDATE OF ((CLEVELAND, 1892), DEMOCRATS)
IS BORN ON ((ROBERT, MILLER), (2, 22, 1935))

The difference in representing PERSONS (by first names and familiy names) and CANDIDATES (by family name only) could arise from the fact that in the declaration of the type PERSON the identifying set includes the two relations HAS FIRST NAME and HAS FAMILY NAME, whereas in the identifying set of the type CANDIDATE only HAS FAMILY NAME is specified as it was found that the family name together with the date at which he was a candidate suffices for identification.

9 The Entity-Relationship Model

The *Entity-Relationship Model* was introduced in [Che 1] as a tool to model real world situations for data base design and usage. In this respect it is similar to the Logical Database Model (LDM) as introduced in the preceding chapter. The entity-relationship model, however, was less formally developed and it relies more on a graphical representation than on fully developed schema definition and data base instance languages. The entity-relationship model (ERM) has found wide acceptance in research communities and many investigations have been based on it. Some of the results have been presented at three Entity-Relationship Conferences, [Che 2, Che 3, and DJNY].

We shall first introduce the Er-model proper and then extend it by abstraction concepts as introduced in [Sa].

In Fig. 9.1 the underlying philosophy of the entity-relationship model is represented. The data base world is structured into levels. The first level deals with entities and relationships, the second with a "graphical" and a "relational" representation of entities and relationships, and finally the third level offers a table format, i.e. relations in the conventional sense, for an access path independent realization in a data base system. Very roughly, the first level could be seen to correspond to the abstract world model and the second level to the logical schema and the logical state description of LDM. When introducing the model, we shall, however, point out some important differences.

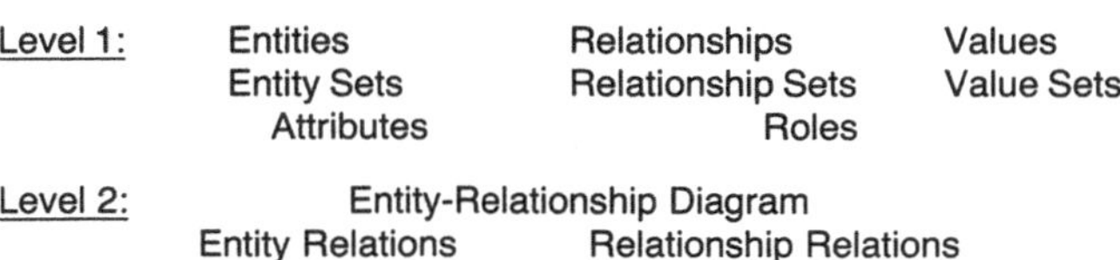

Fig. 9.1. The level structure of the ER Model

9.1 The Entity-Relationship-Value Concept

9.1.1 Level 1: Entities, Relationships, Values

At the Level 1 entities and relationships are the principal concepts. An *entity* is defined as a "thing" which can be distinctly identified. A specific person, a company, an event are examples of entities. A *relationship* is an association among entities, as for example the "father-son" relationship between two "person" entities.

The database contains *relevant information* concerning entities and relationships of interest to the enterprise, i.e. contained in the universe of discourse. A complete description of entities and relationships usually will not be recorded in the database. In most cases, it is unnecessary (if not even impossible) to record every potentially available piece of information about entities and relationships. Some facts of potential interest will always remain outside the data base system. In the logical data base model, this situation was reflected in the statements about non-proveability of the equivalence between the abstract model and the real universe of discourse (which in LDM means *all* information of potential interest to the data base users).

The *entities* in the universe of discourse are classified into different *entity sets* E_i such as "employee", "project", and "department". There is a predicate associated with each entity set, that tests whether an arbitrary entity belongs to the set. Entities may belong to more than one entity set, i.e. entity sets are not mutually disjoint. For example, an entity that belongs to the entity set "male person" also belongs to the entity set "person".

A *relationship set* is a mathematical relation among n entities

$$\{[e_1, e_2, \ldots, e_n] \mid e_1 \in E_1, e_2 \in E_2, \ldots, e_n \in E_n\}$$

and each tuple $[e_1, e_2, \ldots, e_n]$ is a *relationship*. The E_i's and e_i's in the above definition need not be different. The *role* of an entity in a relationship xpresses the function the entity performs in the relationship. In a relationship set "marriage" defined between entities from the entity set "person", e.g.

$$\text{“marriage”} = \{[e_1, e_2] \mid e_1 \in \text{“person”}, e_2 \in \text{“person”}\},$$

the first element in the tuple may appear in the role "husband", the second in the role "wife". In LDM roles were identified by position numbers only, not by additional names.

Additional information about an entity besides entity set predicates and relationships is expressed by a set of *attribute – value pairs* associated with the entity. Examples of *values* are "red", "3", "John", "Miller" etc., and they are classified into mutually disjoint *value sets* such as "color", "feet", "first name", "last name" etc. There is a predicate associated with each value set which tests whether a value belongs to the set. A value in one set may be equivalent (in a real world sense) to a value in a different value set. For example, "12" in value set "inch" is equivalent to "1" in value set "feet".

An *attribute* is defined as a function that maps from an entity set or a relationship set into a value set or a Cartesian product of value sets.

$\text{attr}_1\colon E_i \rightarrow V_{i1} \times V_{i2} \times \ldots \times V_{in}$
$\text{attr}_2\colon R_i \rightarrow V_{i1} \times V_{i2} \times \ldots \times V_{in}$

In Fig. 9.2 the attributes defined on the entity set COMPANY are illustrated. The attribute NAME maps company entities into elements of the value set COMPANY NAME. The attribute ADDRESS maps from the entity set COMPANY into a pair CITY NAME, STREET NAME of value sets. INCOME and CASH, both map from the entity set COMPANY into the value set DOLLAR. Note that an attribute is always defined as a function. Therefore it maps a given entity to a single value respectively tuple if a value set product is identified.

Relationships also may have attributes. In Fig. 9.3 the relationship MACHINE-WORKER is illustrated. The attribute USAGE which defines the number of hours a specific worker e_j uses a machine e_i is an attribute of the corresponding relationship. It is neither an attribute of the WORKER nor the MACHINE entity set since its meaning depends on the relationship between the two, i.e. a pair $[e_i, e_j]$.

We now can try to relate these concepts to the Logical Database Model. Entity sets roughly correspond to the types of LDM, but attributes and value/value-set concepts do not exist in LDM. That is, they are either represented as properties or as relationships. For example the ER-model concept

Entity Set	Attributes	Value Sets
CAR	COLOR	COLOR
$\{e_1, e_2, \ldots\}$		{blue, red, green, ...}

could be represented by the types "blue car", "red car", "green car", or by the two

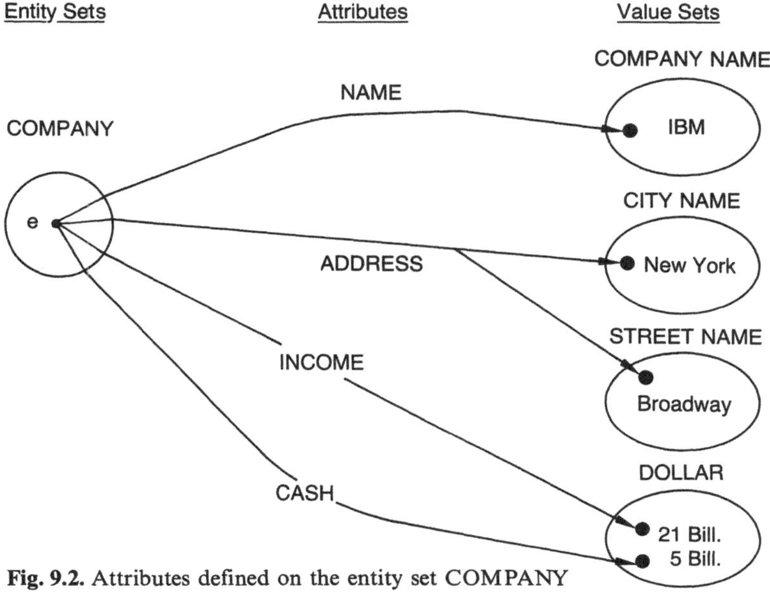

Fig. 9.2. Attributes defined on the entity set COMPANY

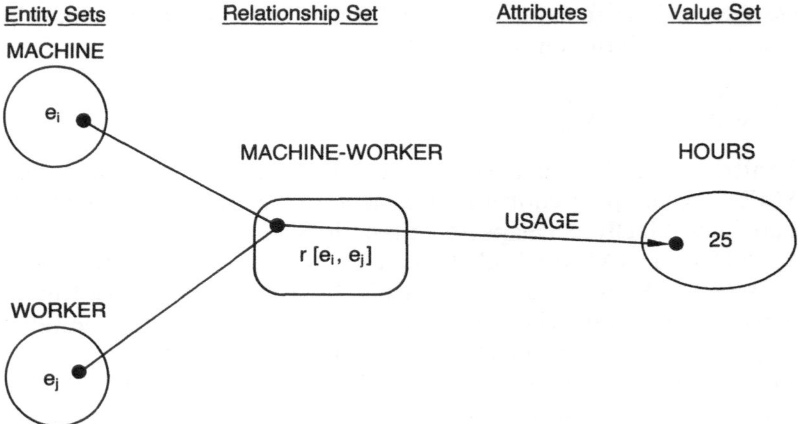

Fig. 9.3. Attributes defined on the relationship set MACHINE-WORKER

types "car", "color" and the relationship "car has color". Using values and value sets has a number of disadvantages which are avoided in LDM:

1) Attributes are only functional mappings. The fact that a car may have more than one color cannot be represented in the above example.
2) The only facts that can be recorded about values in the ER-model is their membership in a value set. If any other property is to be represented, the value has to be changed to an entity. For example, if we want to record the wave length for each color, we cannot do that in the above ER-model, but have first to change the value set COLOR into an entity set.

Values and value sets, however, have the advantage that functions are in general easier understood and reflect more closely the concept that an object, e.g. a car, has associated with it a color, e.g. green. Here "green" is not necessarily seen as an object in its own right but rather as an attribute of the car. Relationships roughly correspond to the relations of LDM, but in LDM relations by themselves cannot have properties or take part in relationships (to model the relationship-attribute concept of the ER-model). For example, the ER relationship of Fig. 3.3 has to be represented by a ternary relation in LDM. We could, for example, introduce "machine used by worker for hours" between the three types "machine", "worker" and "hours". But here we lose the fact that "hours" is really related to an "activity" represented by machine-worker pairs. A better LDM structure would therefore be

Types	*Relations*
T_1: machine	R_1: machine used by worker for activity
T_2: worker	
T_3: activity	R_2: activity has hours
T_4: hour	

where activities appear as entities that are related by R_1 to machines and workers and by R_2 to the hours they last. In this case, the ER-model is able to represent the information more compactly and may be for some persons more naturally.

9.1.2 Level 2: Entity-Relationship Diagram

For the Entity-Relationship Model a graphical representation has been introduced and supplemented by a relational data model oriented interpretation, the *Entity Relations* and *Relationship Relations*. In Fig. 9.4 the *entity-relationship diagram* reflecting information about divisions, division employees and machine usage is presented.

Each entity set is represented by a rectangular box, a relationship by a diamond and a value set by a circle. The roles connecting entity sets to relationship sets are identified by lines as are the attributes connecting value sets to entity respectively relationship sets.

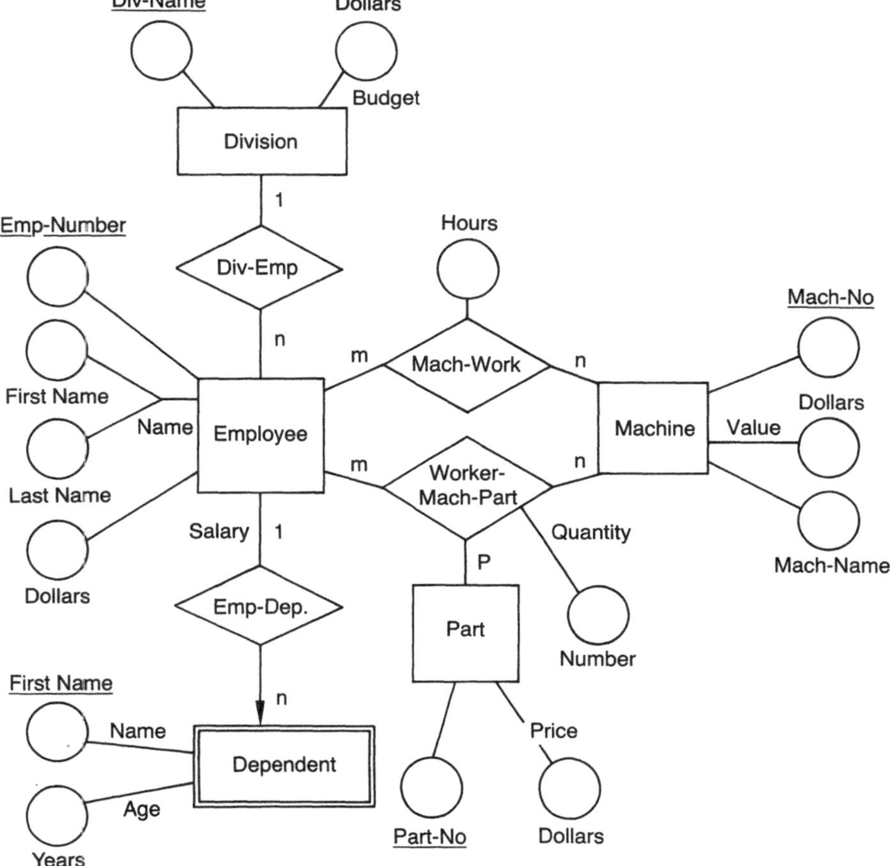

Fig. 9.4. The Entity-Relationship Diagram for the machine usage in divisions

An *entity key* is a group of attributes of an entity that can be used to identify the different entities of an entity set. Formally, an entity key is a group of attributes such that the mapping from the entity set to the corresponding group of value sets is one-to-one. It is possible that more than one such group exists for an entity set, one of these keys is then selected as the *entity primary key*. In the ER-diagram the primary key attributes are identified by underlining the corresponding value sets. The values associated through the primary key with an entity will also be used as the representation of the entity.

9.1.3 Level 3: Entity Relations, Relationship Relations and Relation Tables

To represent entities and their attribute values, a relational table form is used (Fig. 9.5). The representation of the entities here is "integrated" with the representation of the values Emp-Number. As a consequence a change of the value of an Emp-Number is defined to mean a *renaming* of the entity, not a replacement of one entity by another one.

In some cases an entity cannot be uniquely identified by the value of its own attributes. In these cases relationships may be used together with attributes to reach the required one-to-one mapping. In Fig. 9.6 such a *weak entity relation* is illustrated. In the ER-diagram the fact that a DEPENDENT entity is identified by a weak entity relation is illustrated by a double-lined box for the entity set DEPENDENT.

Theoretically, any relationships could be used, as in the Logical Data Model, but the ER-model restricts such relationships to binary relationships with a 1:n mapping, i.e. one "employee" entity may have n "dependent" entities associated), where in addition the existence of entities in the second entity set depends on the *existence* of an associated entity in the first entity set. For example, dependents of an employee can only be in the data base if the employee is. To indicate this *existence dependency* an arrow is used in the corresponding role line.

Relationships are identified and represented through the representation of the entities taking part in the relation. That is, the attributes connected to a relationship are *not* used for representing relationships. In Fig. 9.7 a *relationship relation* is presented that can be used to represent relationships and their associated attribute values. The *relationship primary key* is simply the combination of the primary keys

	Primary Key			
Attributes	Emp-Number	Name		Salary
Value Sets	Emp-Number	First Name	Last Name	Dollars
Entities	15634 48534	John George	Miller Smith	38.000 49.000

Fig. 9.5. The entity relation Employee

	← Primary Key →			
Entity Set	Employee			
Role	Dependent			
Entity Key	Emp-Number	Name	Age	Attributes
Key Value Set	Emp-Number	First Name	Years	Value Sets
Entities	48532	Janet	6	
	48532	Bill	9	
	15634	Maria	3	

Fig. 9.6. The weak entity relation DEPENDENT

of the associated entities. In the graphic representation the role names – which together form the name of the relationship set – are written inside of the diamonds. On the role lines information is specified about the number of entities associated with each other in a relationship. For example, one division entity may have "n" employees associated by the Division-Employee relationship, i.e. there exists a 1 : n mapping from DIVISION to EMPLOYEE. In the relationship set Worker-Machine-Part one employee may work on "n" machines producing "p" parts, or one machine may be worked by "m" employees producing "p" parts, or one part may be produced by "m" employees on "n" machines. Here "m", "n" and "p" do not identify any specific number but just the type of mapping, m:n:p involved in the relationship. In LDM the cardinality restriction roughly corresponds to these indicators, but there a *min* and *max* value for the possible "m", "n" and "p" 's could be specified.

The entity relationship model also proposes a *data definition language* for specifying an ER-schema. The precise syntax of that language is not important here. The language principally allows to transcribe the information contained in an ER-diagram. In addition data types, i.e. representation rules, and value ranges, e.g. 1 to 2000, can be specified for value sets. Constraint specifications have not been formally introduced in the ER-model. Some discussion can be found in [Che 1], but we shall keep our attention in this area on the rather extensive discussion of constraints in the logical data model.

For information retrieval, insertion, deletion, and update a *manipulation language* has been defined only informally for the ER-model, but we shall not

	← Relationship Primary Key		→		
Entity Set	Employee	Machine	Part		
Role	Worker	Machine	Part		
Entity Key	Emp-Number	Mach-No	Part-No	Quantity	Attributes
Key Value Set	Emp-Number	Mach-No	Part-No	Number	Values
Relationships	48532	M5	SK-158	3	
	15634	M8	AJ-597	186	

Fig. 9.7. The relationship relation WORKER-MACHINE-PART

discuss it here as a similar language of more power and completeness will be introduced in Chap. 10.

9.2 Data Types and the Entity-Relationship Model

We shall now extend the basic entity-relationship model by concepts derived from the structuring principles found in data structures and the theory of data types. The extension was proposed in [SNF] and is extensively described in [Sa]. A somewhat more restricted proposal can also be found in [SS].

To unify our terminology we shall call entity sets, relationship sets and value sets types. To obtain more complex types, three constructors are introduced that will be used to produce from some given types new types.

1) *Aggregation* – called *product* in [SNF] – constructs a new entity set out of a relationship set.
2) *Generalization* – called *sum* in [SNF] – allows to form a new entity set by a union of other entity sets. The inverse process is called *specialization* – *subset* in [SNF] – and it splits an entity set into a number of entity sets.
3) *Grouping* – called *correspondence* in [SNF] – defines a new entity set where each entity consists of a group of entities of the source entity set.

From here on we shall refer to the entities, relationships, entity sets and relationship sets constructed in the ER-model without the use of the above operators as *basic types* whenever we want to distinguish them from the general types derivable in the extended ER-model.

As an example of the extended framework let us investigate the diagram of Fig. 9.4 once more. The ternary relationship Worker-Machine-Part represents the idea that an activity in the company is described as "a worker on some machine

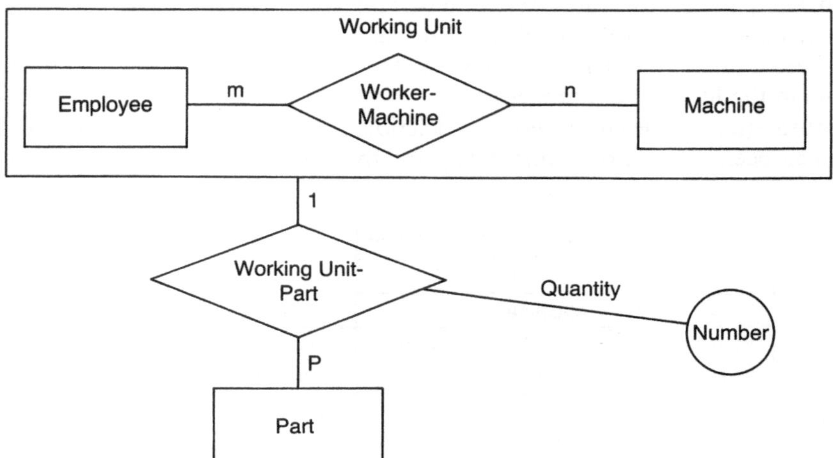

Fig. 9.8. The operation Aggregation in the extended ER-model

producing some specific part in some specific quantity". However, the same situation could be seen somewhat differently. In the company machines could be assigned to workers and this "team" then produces parts in some specified quantity. In the original ER-model this situation could not have been modelled correctly as a relationship cannot be related to another entity or relationship. In the extended model the problem is solved easily (see Fig. 9.8).

We are now even able to record the fact that a specific part can only be produced by a specific working unit ("Team"), i.e. a 1 : p relationship exists between working units and parts. All the other attributes and relationships of Fig. 9.4 remain the same.

Let us now investigate the three operators in some more detail (see also [SNF]).

9.2.1 Generalization/Specialization

If $T_1, T_2, \ldots T_n$ are (generalized) entity sets, a *Generalization* is denoted by

$T_1 \mid T_2 \mid \ldots \mid T_n$

and defines a new entity set T with the meaning

$t \in T \leftrightarrow \exists T_i (1 \leqq i \leqq n \wedge t \in T_i).$

That is, there exists for every entity in T *at least one* T_i which contains that entity.

For example, in our entity-relationship diagram of Fig. 9.4 we could decide that the employees of a company in reality have to be distinguished according to their occupation as secretaries, administrators, and workers. This could not be represented naturally in the ER-diagram and the ER-model. Only through the fact that the entity set worker, for example, is *always* (i.e. at all times) a subset of the entity set employee could we deduce some kind of dependency between the two types. Using the Generalization operation, we could derive from Figs. 9.4 and 9.8 a new ER-diagram as illustrated (partially) in Fig. 9.9. Notice that we have introduced a new additional attribute-value pair for the entity set EMPLOYEE. This attribute allows us to distinguish between the members of the different classes of employees. If we have an entity set EMPLOYEE and want to use the Specialization operator as an inverse to Generalization, we have to specify in the model *roles*, i.e. rules, that define when an EMPLOYEE entity belongs to one or the other component entity set. We therefore generalize the ER-Diagram representation of Generalization/Specialization to the one shown in Fig. 9.10. The rules can be any predicative expressions on the properties (attribute-value pairs and relationships) of the entities considered. If for every employee entity we could always decide to which component entity set(s) it belongs without using the attribute-value pair Job Type, but some other of the properties already represented then, that pair would not have to be introduced. The rules defining the specialization of an entity set are called *Characterizations* of the contained entity sets. For example, Job Type = 1 is the Characterization of the entity set SECRETARY in the entity set EMPLOYEE.

In a Generalization/Specialization the attributes and relationships of the "generalized" entity set are *inherited* by the component entity sets. For example, the

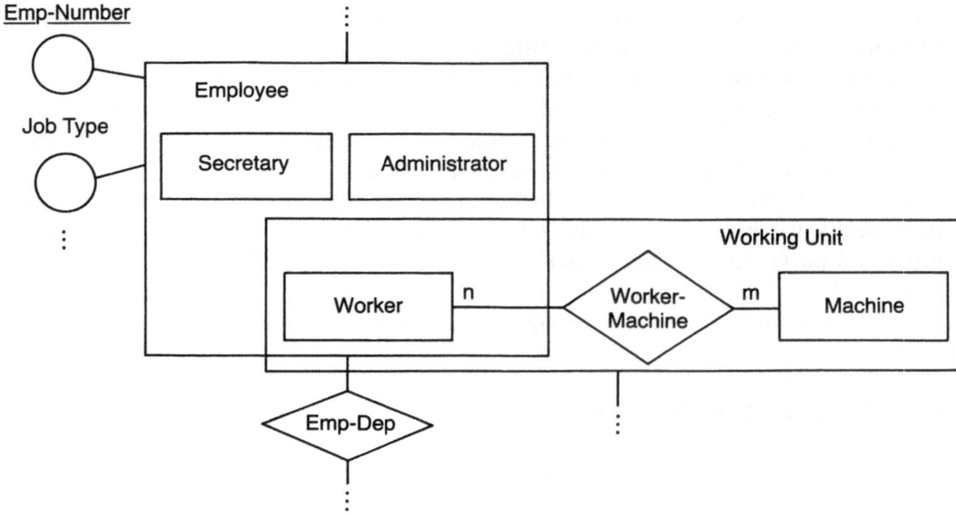

Fig. 9.9. The operation Generalization (and Aggregation) in the extended ER-model

attributes EMP-NUMBER, JOB TYPE, NAME, and SALARY of EMPLOYEE are considered to be also attributes of the entity sets SECRETARY, ADMINISTRATOR and WORKER. The same holds for the relationships Division-Employee and Employee-Dependent. Since we are dealing with the same entities, i.e. real world things, in both the global and component entity sets this property of the Generalization/Specification operation should not be of surprise. Of course, additional attribute-value pairs and relationships could be defined for any component entity set. See Fig. 9.9 for example, where the relationship Worker-Machine now is defined only on the component entity set WORKER of the EMPLOYEE entity set.

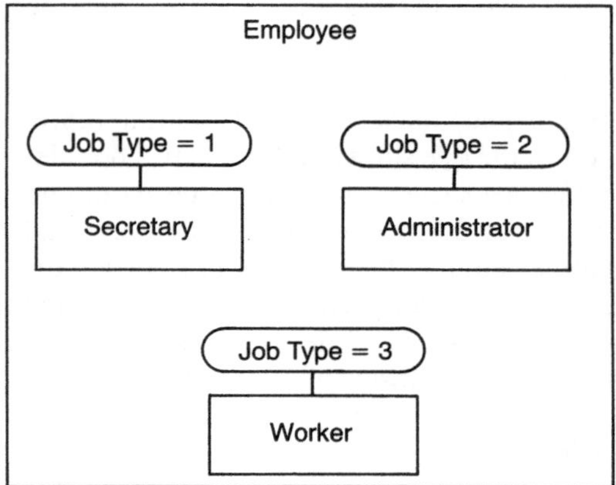

Fig. 9.10. The Generalization/Specialization operation with Characterization

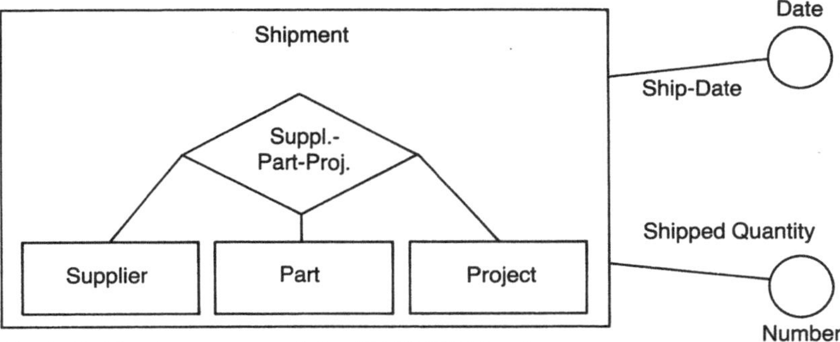

Fig. 9.11. The Aggregation of the SHIPMENT entity set.

9.2.2 Aggregation

The *Aggregation* (an example is shown in Fig. 9.8) is defined by:
If $T_1, T_2, \ldots, T_n$ are (generalized) entity sets, an Aggregation is denoted by

$\langle T_1, T_2, \ldots, T_n \rangle$ or by $\langle s_1 : T_1, s_2 : T_2, \ldots, s_n : T_n \rangle$

where $s_1, s_2, \ldots, s_n$ are called selectors which extract (or project to) one of the component entity sets. The operation defines a new entity set T with the meaning

$$t \in T \longleftrightarrow \exists t_1, t_2, \ldots, t_n (t_1 \in T_1 \wedge t_2 \in T_2 \wedge \ldots \wedge t_n \in T_n \wedge \langle t_1, t_2, t_3, \ldots, t_n \rangle = t)$$

That is, the new entities are formed as *tuples* of entities from the component entity sets. To be meaningful the entity sets $T_1, T_2, \ldots, T_n$ have to be part of some common relationship, and this relationship will always be included in the representation of the generated entity set.

Attribute-value set pairs can be attached to the new entity set. It also can take part in any relationship. Another example of an Aggregation operation is given in Fig. 9.11. The new entity set SHIPMENT is defined as an aggregation of the three entity sets SUPPLER, PART and PROJECT with the new attributes Ship-Date and Shipped-Quantity. There is an important difference between these two attributes, however. While Ship-Date cannot be thought of belonging to any component entity set, the Shipped-Quantity attribute clearly refers to PARTS. Sometimes, e.g. in [RM], this situation is described as: Shipped-Quantity characterizes PARTS with respect to SHIPMENT. We shall call this situation: the attribute Shipped-Quantity is a *characterization* of the entity set PART with respect to SHIPMENT.

9.2.3 Grouping

If T designates some entity set and $T_1, T_2, \ldots, T_n$ are either value sets associated with T or entity sets related via some relationship with T, then the Grouping operator denoted by

$(T_1, T_2, \ldots, T_n)\ \{T\}$

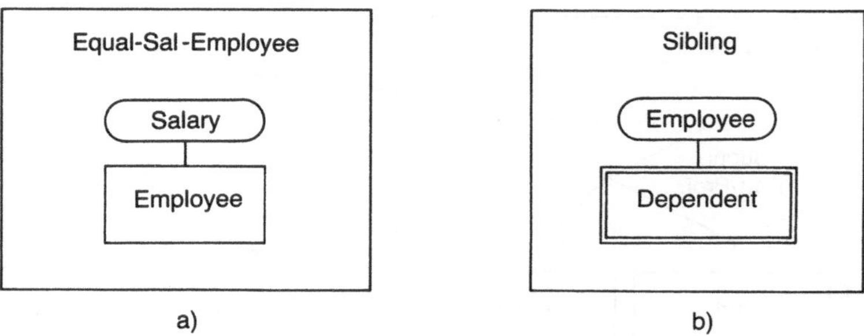

Fig. 9.12 a, b. The Grouping operator of the extended ER-model

constructs a new (grouped) entity set T_G where each element is a set of entities of T such that inside of one such set all entities have the same values and related entities from the entity sets $T_1, T_2, \ldots, T_n$ associated. The types $T_1, T_2, \ldots, T_n$ will be called *indexing types*, T the *basis*.

For example, we may use the Salary-Dollar pair from our example in Fig. 9.4 to construct a grouped-entity set from the EMPLOYEE entity set. In Fig. 9.12 the resulting ER-diagram component is illustrated. Each EMPLOYEE entity in a set of entities representing one entity in EQUAL-SALARIED-EMPLOYEE has the same Salary value.

In Fig 9.12b a related entity, EMPLOYEE, is used to group the DEPENDENT entity set. The entities having the same employee associated by the relationship Employee-Dependent form a new entity in the entity set SIBLING. Fig. 9.13 shows an example where more than one indexing type is used. In this case, the indexing types consist of attribute-value and relationship-entity set pairs to allow a complete identification. The derived entity set contains elements (entities), each consisting of those EMPLOYEE entities that have the same first name and have used the same specific machine for producing parts.

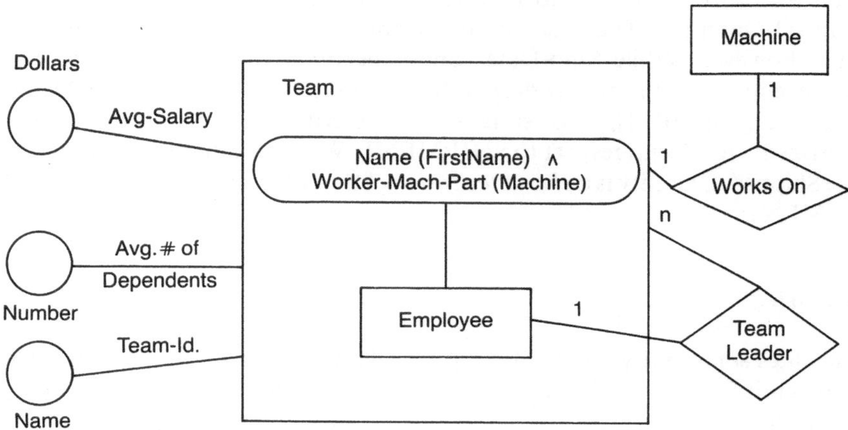

Fig. 9.13. The Grouping operator using more than one grouping criteria

Note that in the last example the relationship Worker-Machine-Part is m:n between employees and machines. As a result the sets of entities in the derived entity set will in general not be disjoint.

We may attach attributes to entity sets that are derived through a Grouping operation, and they may also take part in relationships (see Fig. 9.13).

Two types of relationships can be distinguished when they are associated with entity sets derived through the Grouping operation.

1) Relationships *derived* from the relationship in the indexing entity sets. In our example, this is the relationship Works-On which identifies the machine which has been used by the specific group. Because of the properties of the grouping operator these relations are always binary and 1:1.
2) Relationships *inherent* to the derived entity set itself. An example is the relation Team-Leader which identifies the leader of a team. Note that the relationship allows for an employee to lead more than one team. In addition, the team leader is not restricted to be a member of the team. Additional constraints would have to be specified to achieve this goal.

In case of attributes, it is also possible to distinguish between two situations:

1) Attributes *derived* from the attributes and relationships of the basis. Examples are the Average-Salary of all employees in a team and the Average-Number of their dependents. Following the path through a relationship, we could even define a derived attribute Average-Age of the dependents in each team.
2) Attributes *inherent* to the derived entity set. In Fig. 9.13 the Team-Identification is such an attribute. It can be used to uniquely identify a team, that is it could be selected as the entity key of the derived entity set TEAM.

9.3 Existence and Indentification Constraints in the Extended ER-Model

Adapting the notion of characteristic and identifying sets introduced in [BN2] and discussed in Sect. 8.2 to the extended ER-model we shall say that a *component* is *characteristic in* a *construct* if its presence is required for the existence of the construct. Inversely, the *construct* is *characteristic for* a *component* if its presence is required for the existence of the component.

An *identifying set*, as in Sect. 8.2, establishes the individuality of objects and forms the basis for the objects' representation in the data base.

We shall now investigate these notions with respect to the ER-model and especially the three type-building operations introduced in Sect. 8.2.

9.3.1 Constraints Related to Generalization/Specialization

Whenever a Generalization/Specialization operation is used, an entity may belong to different entity sets that can be seen as being arranged in a hierarchy. For example, the entity sets

a) PERSON
b) EMPLOYEE
c) SECRETARY

form successively lower, i.e. more specialized, levels of an entity set hierarchy.

A reasonable rule of existence would be that for an entity set at level i all the entity sets at levels j ($i < j \leqq$ top level) are characteristic. That is, an entity existing at level i also must exist at all higher levels. Inversely, if an entity is eliminated from an entity set at level i, it must also cease to exist at any lower level.

As to identification, one must be able to differentiate entities belonging to the different component entity sets of a Generalization/Specialization. For example, the identifying sets of WORKER and SECRETARY may only be identical if at least one of the components of the set contains some characteristic values or relationships which distinguish secretaries from workers. In Fig. 3.9, for example, the identifying sets of SECRETARIES, ADMINISTRATORS, and WORKERS could be

{Emp-Number, Job Type}

if in Job Type every secretary has a code different from administrators and workers and vice versa. If such a component does not exist, the identifying sets of SECRETARIES, ADMINISTRATORS and WORKERS would have to contain differing value sets respectively relationship sets.

9.3.2 Constraints Related to Aggregation

An Aggregation operator constructs an entity set out of a relationship set. For that reason, this entity set behaves very similar to the underlying relationship set. For example, for irreducible relations (in the terminology of Chap. 8) all the entity sets taking part in the relationship set will normally be characteristic to the construct. For example, for the SHIPMENT entity set of Fig. 9.11 the SUPPLIER, PART, and PROJECT entity sets will be characteristic. The inverse of course will not be true. Suppliers may exist that do not supply any project, they are only "kept on file" for later reference, and so on. However, if company policy says that somebody is a supplier only if he actually supplies parts to some project, then the SHIPMENT entity set will be characteristic for the SUPPLIER entity set.

For the identification of an entity in an entity set derived by an aggregation, normally the same strategy will be followed as for the underlying relationship set. That is, an element will be identified using the identifying sets of the component entities. However, it is possible to introduce for the derived entity set its own identifying attribute-value set pairs or relationship sets. For example we could attach in Fig. 9.11 a new attribute-value pair

(Shipment number : number)

which could be unique within a specific day. Then an identifying set for the SHIPMENT entity set would be

{Ship Date, Shipment number}

replacing the combination, e.g. Supplier No., Part No., and Project No., as the entity primary key for SHIPMENT.

9.3.3 Constraints Related to Grouping

For entity sets derived by Grouping there is a strong tendency that all components of the indexing set are characteristic. On the other hand, the basis, i.e. the entity set used for forming the groups, is only characteristic in the sense that for each existing "grouped" entity in the derived entity set at least one entity has to exist in the basis. The inverse is not required, i.e. there is no need that every entity in the basis set is a member of some entity in the derived set.

The derived entity set of a Grouping operation is usually identified by the indexing set. That is, the indexing set is the identifying set. If no other identifying set exists for the derived entity set, this set will become the entity primary key.

For example, in Fig. 9.13 the identifying set

{Name (First Name), Worker-Machine-Part (Machine)}

for TEAM is equivalent to the indexing set. But the TEAM entity set also has the attribute value set pair

Team-Id: Name

which also forms an identifying set

{Team-Id (Name)}

and this would produce simpler identifying values when chosen as the entity primary key of the TEAM entity set.

In the identifying set of the components of derived types the attribute value set pairs and the relationship sets of the higher entities may play a role. An example can be seen in Fig. 3.12. The DEPENDENT-entity set will have an identifying set and entity primary key

{Emp-Number, Name (First Name)}

where the Emp-Number is the entity primary key for the SIBLING entity set and Name (First Name) an attribute value set pair of the DEPENDENT entity set.

9.4 An Example Using the Extended ER-Model

The example (Fig. 9.14) is derived from Fig. 9.4 and the various examples introduced with the extended ER-model in Sect. 9.2.

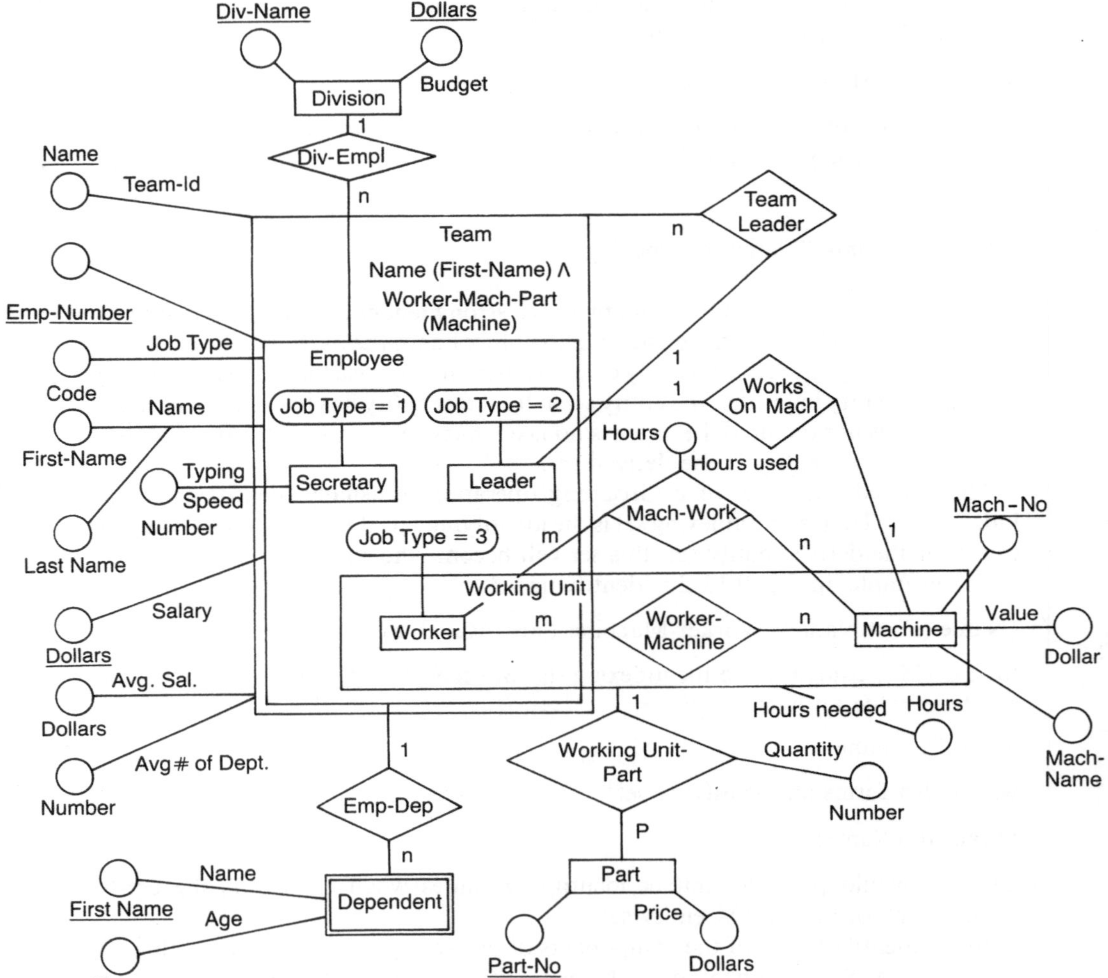

Fig. 9.14. The extended ER-Model of Company Divisions

We believe from all that has been said before, the example to be self explanatory. However, we want to make a general remark here. As can be seen from even such a simple situation, the Entity Relationship Diagrams rapidly became voluminous and hard to read. As a consequence, a computerized graphic support tool would be of high value. Such tools have been developed but the orientation of this book and space limitations prevent us from going into this very interesting and important subject of semantic data models.

10 The Temporal Hierarchic Model

The *Temporal Hierarchic Model* (THM) was developed at the University of Stuttgart. It is based on the results and principles explained in Chap. 8 (The Logical Database Model) and 9 (The ER-Model), but extends them considerably by adding among others

a) time aspects,
b) abstract data type concepts

to the modelling technique.

THM is described in detail in a number of publications, e.g. [Sc1, Sc2, SFNC, HS, Wa], and more formally in [Sc3], not only with respect to its language and graphic representation, but also as a development tool to be used in information systems design. In this book, we are not able to cover all aspects of THM and therefore will concentrate only on the time aspects and the abstract data type concepts. As a graphical notation, we shall use the facilities of the Entity Relationship Diagram and adjust them to THM where necessary. To explain the concepts we shall, as in the other chapters of this book, rely mainly on examples. Sometimes we take the freedom to change the names of some of the concepts of THM to make them fit better into our framework.

10.1 The Basic Concepts of THM

Like the Logical Database Model and the Entity Relationship Model the Temporal Hierarchic Model is based on the concept of *entity* as an abstraction of real world objects. *Classes* are sets of entities that have some common characteristics. Like entity sets in the ER-model and types in LDM classes need not be disjoint.

Two types of *relations* are introduced in THM:

1) *class relations* which hold between a class and some other classes and/or entities of the model, and
2) *member relations* which hold between the members of classes i.e. between entities.

The second concept corresponds to relationship sets in the ER-model and relations in LDM. The first concept does not exist in these models. It allows the specification of characteristics for whole classes and not only for the members thereof. For

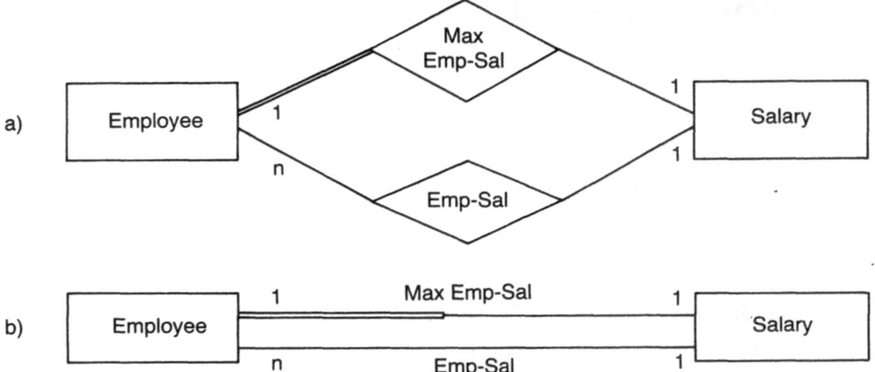

Fig. 10.1 a, b. Class relations and number relations of THM

example, if we would like to specify the maximum salary of all employees in a company, then a relation between the class EMPLOYEE and a SALARY entity has to be established. In Fig. 10.1 a a graphic representation of this situation is given, illustrating also the member relation Employee-Salary. Notice, the double line used in the class relation to identify that a whole class and not its member entities are involved in it.

The THM does not use the attribute-value set concepts of the ER-model. Instead, attribute value set pairs have to be expressed via classes and relations. Therefore, it is also possible to delete the diamond symbol in the diagrams and to represent relationships by lines only (Fig. 10.1 b). We shall use both notations interchangeably to simplify our diagram.

Before continuing with additional concepts of THM, let us investigate once more the idea of class relations. Maximum salary is just one property of the EMPLOYEE class we may want to express in our model. Actually, employees could have a maximum age, an average salary etc. attached. These we formerly could only express for *entities* that by themselves were sets of entities again. In THM a class is not considered to be an entity proper, that is, it is not necessary to apply the Grouping operator of the extended ER-model to EMPLOYEE. Using the Grouping operator in this case would seem unnatural as we *always* would end up with an entity set containing a single element, i.e. the set of all employees. The class relation offers even other advantages. In Fig. 10.2 we have expressed properties of a class that normally are considered to be characteristics included in the declaration of the class and that represent range definitions, data type specifications, constraints etc. As a consequence, we are now able to talk about such properties in the same way as about properties of entities. In such a way we have unified the treatment of "schema" properties and "instance" properties, as has been done for a long time in the field of artificial intelligence. Normally, in the data base field schema properties are considered to be rather static in their behaviour – they only change when the schema changes, and then they are changed by a "data definition"

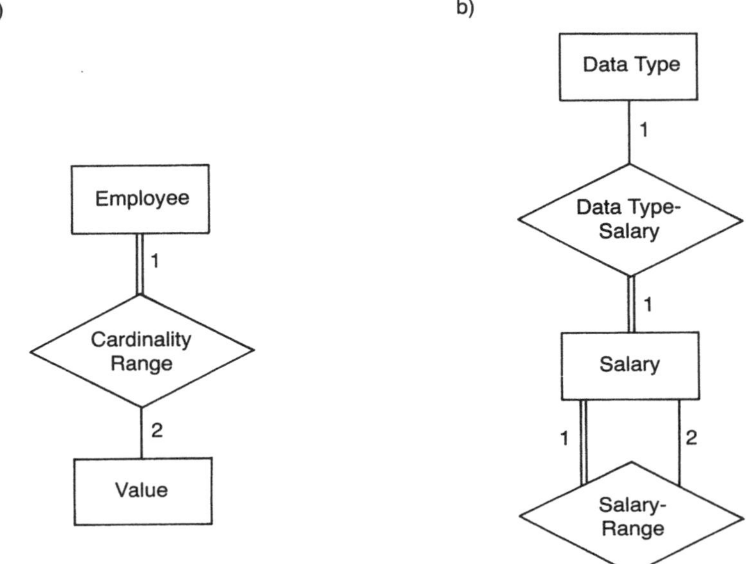

Fig. 10.2 a, b. Class relationships used for "Schema" properties

language and not by the "data manipulation" language. In THM these differences disappear and a more homogeneous view of the world develops.

The Temporal Hierarchic Model also uses concepts of

1) Generalization/Specification,
2) Aggregation, and
3) Grouping

introduced for the extended ER-model in [SNF] and [SS] and discussed in Chap. 9.2. All the characteristics of those operations remain the same when applied to the TH-model, and we therefore just give an example (Fig. 10.3) which is a simple adaption of Fig. 9.13 to THM. Notice that attribute-value set pairs are replaced by relation-class pairs, and that relations are sometimes expressed by a line, sometimes, for enhancement reasons, using a diamond. A class relation Max-Salary has been added. It establishes the relationship between all employees (i.e. the class EMPLOYEE) and the maximum salary (i.e. a SALARY entity) that currently exists in the data base.

10.2 The Notions of Time in THM

So far THM and the other models discussed here only allow us to specify a static, structural presentation of the objects, properties and relationships of the unverse of discourse. However, an information system must have activities that can be applied to the structures to retrieve, update, insert and destroy the different components of

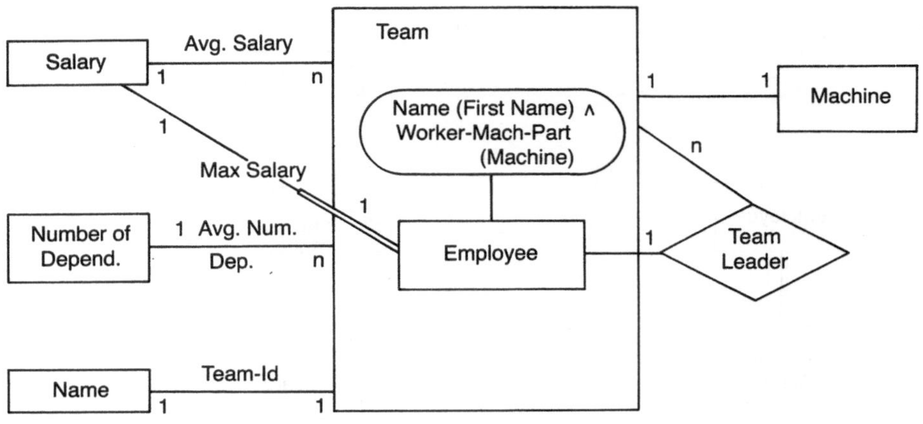

Fig. 10.3. The Grouping operator in THM

the model. These activities always will have to take place in some time frame, as they can only be seen to transform a current instance of the information model into some "next" instance thereof. Immediately, it becomes clear that time aspects will have to become part of the model if the proper behaviour of the activities is to be expressed at all.

THM introduces the *clock* as a special class which, by some mechanism outside of the model always contains precisely one entity – the *current time*. In addition, it will

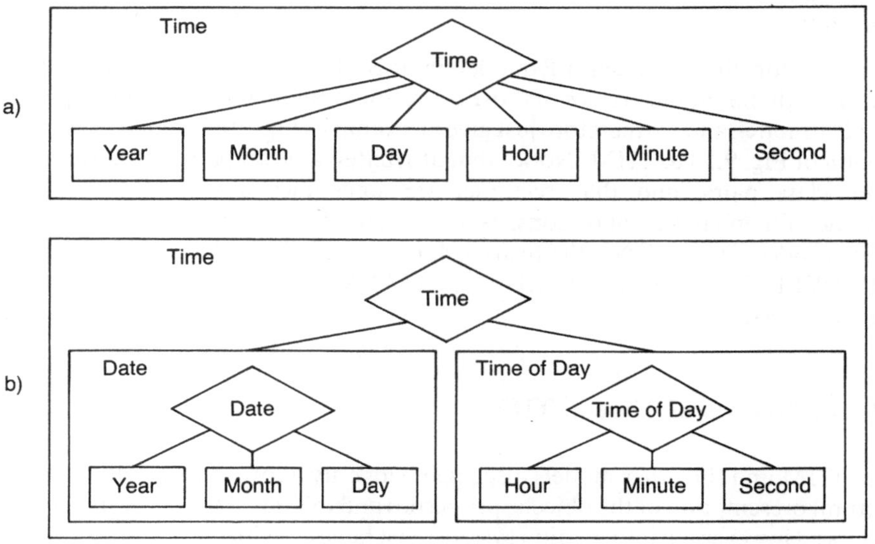

Fig. 10.4a, b. Time classes in the TH-model

normally be necessary to define at least one class, which may be structured, that contains as entities all imaginable time elements. For example, a class Time could be defined as illustrated in Fig. 10.4a and Fig. 10.4b.

We could then use the entities of this class in relations with other entities to express, for example, creation time of an entity, time of change, insertion time into a class, time a relationship is established etc. Using two entities of TIME, we could even express duration (from – to) for entities or relations. The class TIME actually is not different at all from any other class established in the model.

The only other concept concerning time in THM that we want to address here is the important property of "keeping history". Frequently, when an entity is eliminated from a class or a relation element is eliminated from a relation, we need to keep the fact that the entity was part of the class or that such a relationship existed for later referencing purposes. An example would be an employee that leaves a company, but the company still wants to keep a record about the employment. THM provides a special mechanism, called *history-classes*, to keep this information. In Fig. 10.5 this feature of THM is used in connection with an EMPLOYEE class adapted from Figs. 9.4 and 9.14 by replacing attribute value set pairs with class constructs and relations. Some of the relationships of EMPLOYEE and the class EMPLOYEE itself are marked with the symbol "H", meaning "history".

Whenever an entity is deleted from such a class it and the tuples that are connected to it via the marked relations are incorporated into the *history environment* together with an additional relation between the TIME class and the involved entity. In Fig. 10.6, a THM-Diagram illustrates a history environment that would accommodate the above history-class requirements. Notice, that by connecting the entities via a Delete-Time relation to the time class a time stamping mechanism is supplied that allows, at a later point of time, to retrieve the specific situation that

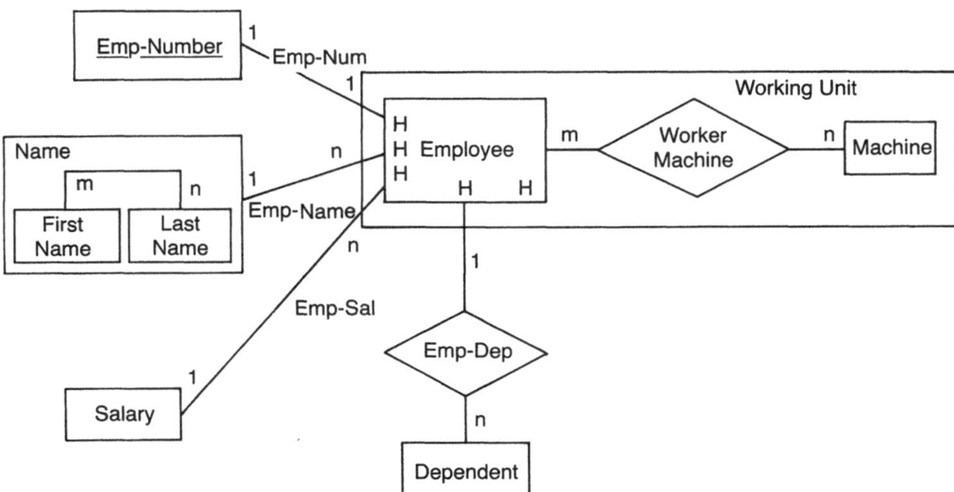

Fig. 10.5. The History-class Indicators in THM-Diagrams

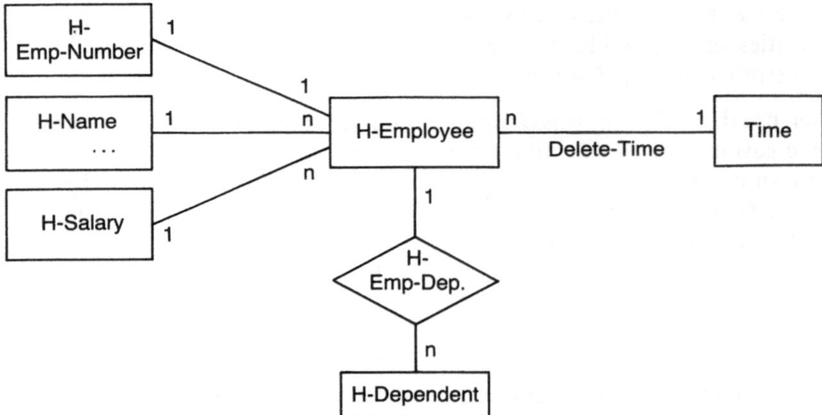

Fig. 10.6. The history environment of THM

existed when that entity was deleted from the EMPLOYEE class. This time stamp even enables us to include multiple deletes of the same entity into a history class. For example, an employee could leave a company, be hired again and leave again. To be able to distinguish the different entries, however, the Delete-Time relation has to be included into the entity primary key (in ER terminology) or the identifying set (in LDM terminology) of the class.

In general, the definition of history is such that the entity deleted and the corresponding elements of the marked relations are incorporated into the history environment, but no further deletes will take place automatically. That is, the deletion of an employee from the EMPLOYEE class will *not* delete its Emp-number from the EMP-NUMBER class. Actions and Activities as discussed in the next section are required to achieve such deletions which of course are necessary if we want to keep our data base states consistent.

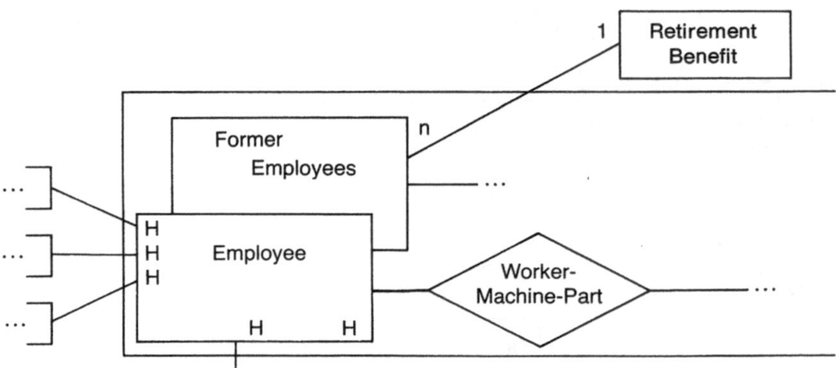

Fig. 10.7. Explicit history classes in a THM-Diagram

The history environment of a THM will normally not be shown explicitly. It is introduced only through the "H"-markings of the various THM components. It is, however, possible to identify some or all components of the history environments in the THM as illustrated in Fig. 10.7. This enables us to explicitly refer to the "old" entities and incorporate them into the other components of the model. Further discussion of the time features in THM can be found in the references [Sc1, Sc2, Sc3, SFNC].

10.3 The Operational Facilities of the Temporal Hierarchic Model

The THM as any other semantic data model tries to represent the information contents of a data base system in such a way as to allow an easy interpretation of the appearing components in the universe of discourse. We have discussed these aspects in detail in Chap. 8 but have excluded from that discussion the aspects of information manipulation that will take place in any data base system that is actually used in some application.

In any semantic model, i.e. the THM here, we should be able to express rules concerning such changes explicitly in order to

a) guide the data base administrator in implementing the model as a real data base system, and
b) allow (automatic) maintenance and control of the static and dynamic consistency of the model and therefore the data base system.

In the discussion of this section we shall concentrate mostly on the dynamic consistency aspects. Static consistency was investigated extensively for LDM (Chap. 8) and the rules and aspects developed there could easily be adapted for THM.

Two different approaches can be distinguished when developing and using dynamic consistency checking mechanisms:

1) General rules are specified that restrict for a given abstract state of the model (we shall use for the moment LDM terminology) the set of possible states that can be reached. Applied recursively, we actually specify via these rules *all imaginable* well formed state transition sequences that would be allowed in the data base system.
2) All allowed actions on the abstract model are specified a priori. With additional rules it is ensured that such actions will only be applied to those abstract states where it is ensured that a "well-formed" abstract state is produced as a result. Here even when applying the definitions recursively, we would not get all imaginable well formed state transition sequences, but only those that can be produced via the a priori specified actions. Other imaginable well formed actions would not be considered by such an approach.

At the first moment, the first approach looks preferable. However, if we analyse it, it turns out that we would have to specify *now* general rules that somehow select in all future from all the imaginable actions only those that will be applicable at a specific point of time and reject at that point of time all the others. Since an unlimited number of such actions may exist, the problem to define such rules looks formidable if not outright impossible. (We assume here that the checking could be done dynamically via tryout/backout approaches. Static checks would clearly belong to the class of undecidable problems as such checks could be reduced to proofs of equivalence between Turing machines).

The second approach at first looks much more restrictive than the first as it requires an a priori definition of activities. But two aspects have to be kept in mind:

a) The approach does not restrict the complexity of an action. Such an action could be a simple insert or retrieve, but it could also be a program calculating the pay checks for some company. It only requires that we think first about what we want to do with a data base and then do it. In most applications of data bases a goal strongly desired.
b) In practice, the approach does not limit the activities that can be performed on the data base. New actions can be defined, in the same way as new classes, relations etc. can be introduced into the data base model. However, here we develop by such modifications a new data base model, whereas in the first approach, the model would not be affected by defining some (new) activities for the data base system. Since in general not every user is allowed to change a data base model and data base schema, a more controlled environment results. Again an approach strongly recommended by software engineering considerations.

However, we want to stress here, that general consistency rules (as given by approach one) will still play an important role in semantic data base modelling. But not in the sense that they are used to check all data manipulations for consistency. Instead, they could guide the designer of new data base actions to develop only "wellformed" activities. They could also be used to check a new activity for "correctness" in the sense that if such an activity is applicable to an abstract state, it is guaranteed that the result state does not violate anyone of the general consistency rules. This does not have to be a complete check. The designer of the data base model in principle is responsible to develop only "correct" models, that is models that correctly reflect the universe of discourse, both from the information representation (entities, classes, relations) and the information manipulation (actions) aspect. As a consequence the rules could be restricted to express only "basic" consistency principles, i.e. rules that are of high importance for the enterprise using the data base system. For example it could be stated that employee descriptions may never be destroyed in the company data base even if they already have left the company for a long time, or a truck driver cannot remain in that position if he should lose his driver's licence. (Notice, the first one is a dynamic, the second a static consistency constraint).

From the preceding discussion it is clear that the second approach is preferable for semantic data base modelling and also that that approach closely corresponds to the programming language concept of abstract data types as introduced and discussed, for example, in [Z] and [Gu].

For the Temporal Hierarchic Model the *abstract data type* approach was chosen. It is described in detail in [Sc1, Sc3, SFNC]. Here we shall base our presentation mostly on examples to illustrate the main dynamic modelling features available in THM.

Introducing abstract data types into a semantic modelling mechanism requires two steps.

1) *Basic actions* have to be defined which provide the basic building blocks for more complex constructs. They could be seen to correspond to the normal statements in a programming language that contains abstract data types.
2) Concepts and *construction rules* have to be introduced that allow the definition of abstract data types in the TH-model.

The actions that we are going to investigate are those concerned with manipulating abstract states, i.e. the instances of the data base schema and not the schema itself. Those other activities comprise a schema definition language which in the framework of our discussions would just be the language used to construct Temporal Hierarchic Diagrams.

An important concept of all manipulation actions is the time stamping mechanism introduced in Sect. 10.2.

Whenever a simple or complex action is specified, a parameter ⟨time⟩ of the form

a) *with time*, or
b) *with time* ⟨time name⟩, or
c) *with* ⟨time name⟩

can be given. At execution time of the activity case a) causes the current entry of *clock* to be taken and used in the operation as specified by the operation semantics. Case b) in addition establishes a name ⟨time name⟩ for that entity, for later usage, e.g. in the individual actions inside of a complex manipulation. Case c) specifies such a usage of the TIME entity.

Some examples are:

delete Employee "John Smith" *with* Comp. Reorg. Time to delete the employee "John Smith" from the class EMPLOYEE using in the history environment the TIME entity identified by Comp. Reorg. Time.

increase salary (Secretaries, Workers) *with time* to increase the salary of all secretaries and workers. Here the TIME entity identified by *with time* can be used inside of this complex activity. Note, that the definition of *increase salary* has to contain a component, e.g. "*with time* Sal Increase" which gives a name to the TIME entity for later use by more basic actions inside of *increase salary*.

10.3.1 The Basic State Manipulation Actions

Depending on the THM construct involved different basic actions will be provided. The principal philosophy followed in introducing these actions tries to provide only minimal "semantics" with each action. For example, to enter an entity by using the *insert*-action, as defined below, into a class constructed by a generalization, it is neither verified that the entity already exists in one of the subclasses nor is the entity inserted into any of those subclasses. That is, as a consequence of a basic *insert*-action consistency constraints of the THM-model may be violated.

This strategy of introducing only "very basic" actions seems to be justified, since a "consistent" insert for a class or group of classes can always be created through the use of the abstract data type facilities. The increase in flexibility but also in understanding of what effects will respectively should occur when an action is performed on the data base justifies, in our opinion, the "additional" work caused by the explicit definition of consistent "higher level" actions.

Manipulation of Entities

create ⟨entity primary key⟩ [⟨time⟩]
The action creates a *new* entity which will be identified by the given ⟨entity primary key⟩. If ⟨time⟩ is specified, the entity will be associated with the TIME entity provided through the construct. The new entity is *not* entered into any class or relation by the create action. The entities referenced in the ⟨entity primary key⟩ must already exist in the current abstract state. To avoid circularity we assume a set of *basic classes*, e.g. Integer, String, Real, where all the members are assumed to exist a priori and to have a commonly understood representation (see the basic types of LDM in Chap. 8).

destroy ⟨entity primary key⟩ [⟨time⟩]
The action destroys the entity identified by the ⟨entity primary key⟩ value. To be wellformed, the entity has to be removed before from any class or relation. The entities referred to in the entity primary key are not affected. The *history environment* is only affected by the actions if ⟨time⟩ is specified. Then the entity will be marked with the TIME entity provided in the History environment.

exist ⟨entity primary key⟩
The action returns the result *true* if the entity identified by the primary key exists in the current THM-state.

Note: If an entity is created and destroyed, another create action with the same entity primary key will create the *same* entity again. If ⟨time⟩ is specified it may have a different create time, but in all other aspects it will be identical to the original one. For the *existence* action we assume some universal knowledge of what entities exist in the current THM-state, but it is left open how such a facility would be implemented in the underlying conventional data base system.

Manipulation of Classes

insert ⟨class⟩ ⟨entity primary key⟩ [⟨time⟩ ⟨time relation⟩]
The entity identified by the primary key is incorporated into the specified class. If a ⟨time relation⟩ is specified, the time element ⟨time⟩ is used to establish a tuple in the relation, whereby, if necessary, a new element may be inserted into the time class referenced through ⟨time relation⟩.

delete ⟨class⟩ ⟨entity primary key⟩ [⟨time⟩]
The entity is deleted from the specified class. If *History* is defined for the class in the THM-model, the entity will be automatically entered with the time ⟨time⟩ into the

history version of the class. Notice that no automatic deletes from relations or higher level classes are performed. Complex operations have to be defined to ensure consistency, even correct time keeping in the history environment, if some relations of the class are marked "H", i.e. are to be kept for later reference in the history environment.

is-element ⟨class⟩ ⟨entity primary key⟩
The value *true* is produced if the entity specified is a member of ⟨class⟩.

Manipulation of Relations

establish ⟨relation⟩ ({⟨entity primary key⟩}$^+$) [⟨time⟩ ⟨time relation⟩]
The tuple of entities specified by the list of primary keys is incorporated in the specified relation. If a ⟨time relation⟩ is specified the time element defined by ⟨time⟩ is used to establish a tuple in that relation, whereby if necessary a new TIME element may be inserted into the class referenced by ⟨time relation⟩. No other entities will be inserted into classes by the *establish* action, i.e. all entities identified by the ⟨entity primary key⟩ list must already be elements of the corresponding classes. If the relation takes part in an Aggregation operation, the entity of that class will be produced as a side effect by the *establish* action.

remove ⟨relation⟩ ({⟨entity primary key⟩ [⟨time⟩]}$^+$) [⟨time⟩]
The relation tuple specified by the ⟨entity primary key⟩ list will be deleted from the relation and automatically entered into the history-version of the class. The TIME entities identified by the ⟨time⟩ specification next to a primary key are used to establish a time stamp for those entities whereas the ⟨time⟩ specified for the whole action establishes a time stamp for the deleted tuple. If the relation takes part in an Aggregation operation, the corresponding entity in that class will be deleted as a side effect of the remove action.

is-element ⟨relation⟩ ({⟨entity primary key⟩}$^+$)
The value *true* is produced if the tuple specified is an element of ⟨relation⟩.

Event Manipulation

raise ({⟨event name⟩}$^+$) [⟨condition⟩]
The action waits until ⟨condition⟩ is satisfied. It then raises all the events identified by the ⟨event name⟩ list.

wait ({⟨event name⟩}$^+$)
The action waits for the occurrence of the specified events. After all events have been raised, the execution of the action sequence that contains the *wait* is continued. If more than one wait action in the system waits for the same event, only one of them will use the event-raising instance. The choice is made randomly (non deterministic).

Retrieval actions

To retrieve elements from the data base state (without changing the state itself) a *query-facility* is provided. A set of entities or a set of relation tuples may be retrieved. The language is based on predicate calculus and will not be discussed further.

(1)	*insert*	Emp-Number Integer (15308)
(2)	*create*	Employee (Emp-Number (15308))
(3)	*insert*	Employee Emp-Number (15308) *with time*
(4)	*insert*	First Name String ('John')
(5)	*insert*	Last Name String ('Miller')
(6)	*insert*	Salary Number (35000.00)
(7)	*establish*	Emp-Number (Emp-Number (15308)) Employee (Emp-Number (15308))
(8)	*establish*	Name (First Name ('John') Last Name ('Miller'))
(9)	*establish*	Emp-Name (Name (First Name ('John') Last Name ('Miller')) Employee (Emp-Number (15308)))
(10)	*establish*	Salary (Salary (35000.00)) Employee (Emp-Number (15308))
(11)	*establish*	Worker-Machine (Employee (Emp-Number (15308)) Machine (Machine Number (M29)))

Fig. 10.8. Establishing EMPLOYEE information by using Basic actions.

Note: Wherever in the definition of basic actions (except in create) an ⟨entity primary key⟩ specification occurs, a query expression can be substituted as long as it is ensured that the result of the query at execution time is just a single entity. This entity will then be used during the action execution.

Using the example of Fig. 10.5 we establish EMPLOYEE information for a new employee using the sequence of actions illustrated in Fig. 10.8.

The notation used for the entity primary keys is adapted from [BN2] and the LD-model. If we use the rules given there for simplifying the primary key representation, we get the operation sequence shown in Fig. 10.9. In both cases, however, the number of basic actions is considerable. Using basic period actions of the kind introduced here is only justifiable because, via abstract data type definitions, more complex actions can be defined and used instead throughout the data base system.

(1)	*insert*	Emp-Number 15308
(2)	*create*	Employee (15308)
(3)	*insert*	Employee 15308 *with time*
(4)	*insert*	First Name 'John'
(5)	*insert*	Last Name 'Miller'
(6)	*insert*	Salary 35000.00
(7)	*establish*	Emp-Number (15308 15308)
(8)	*establish*	Name ('John' 'Miller')
(9)	*establish*	Emp-Name (('John' 'Miller') 15308)
(10)	*establish*	Salary (35000.00 15308)
(11)	*establish*	Worker-Machine (15308 M29)

Fig. 10.9. Establishing EMPLOYEE Information using the simplified notation of LDM

```
action <action name> escape <escape action>
  [start event <event name list>;] [with time <time name>:]
  input <parameter list>;
  output <parameter list>;
  precondition <condition>;
  postcondition <condition>;
  procedure
      [<local action definitions>]*
      <procedure body>
  end.
```

Fig. 10.10. The structure of complex state manipulation actions

10.3.2 Complex State Manipulation Actions

The Temporal Hierarchic Model provides mechanisms to define complex (high level) state manipulation actions using the principles of abstract data types, e.g. [Z, Gu] and of application system design mechanisms as introduced in [St1, St2] and further developed in [Ho].

The general structure of a *complex state manipulation action* (*a complex action*) is illustrated in Fig. 10.10.

Only a single action is defined by the given module structure. In general, abstract data types would allow multiple operations to be defined at that point, but so far such a mechanism has not been provided in the temporal hierarchic model. Because of the impact on consistency constraints the import of abstract data types into an action is currently not controlled, but all actions are assumed to be globally available. In the future, careful restrictions of this facility may become necessary. We shall now discuss the various components contained in the definition of a complex action. We will not give the precise syntax and semantics, but rely on illustrative examples (see Fig. 10.11 for the complex action *insert employee*).

Actions may either be executed by *calling* them or they may be initiated by the occurrence of one or more events. The *start event* clause specifies a list of event names. As soon as all these events have been raised (and have not been taken "away" by some other action), the action will start executing. The *start event* clause here works completely analogous to the basic action *wait* (see Sect. 10.3.1).

The *with time* clause, if present, causes at the time the action is started the *clock* entity to be established as the value of ⟨time name⟩. This value then becomes usable inside of the action.

In the *input* clause two types of input items can be identified.

a) Entities extracted from the current data base state. To define the values general *retrieval actions* as introduced in the preceding section can be used.
b) Entities given to the action by a *parameter passing* mechanism. *Default values* may be established for such parameters by specifying a data base retrieval action which will be used if no value is passed to the parameter at activation time.

As an example of b) with a default value let us consider

mno *of* Machine Number *default*
  mno $\in$ {mano | (($\exists$ emp) (Worker-Machine (emp, mano) *and*
  ($\exists$ div) (Div-Emp (div, emp) *and* Div Name (div) = "Plant")))}

which could be specified instead of the simple

mno *of* Machine Number

in Fig. 10.11. If no machine number is supplied at activation time of *insert employee* the retrieval activity selects one of the machines used in the division named "Plant" and supplies its number to the action.

In the *output parameter list* the entities returned to the outside world via the *parameter passing* mechanism are identified. Components inserted into the data base are not specified explicitly. They will still be available to the outside world as the database state is seen to be globally defined. This corresponds to the external storage features in conventional programming languages which also cannot be hidden inside of modules and abstract data types. Implicitly, the database state output of an action will be controlled by the postcondition clause (see below).

The *precondition* clause specifies with the help of a predicate expression the conditions that have to be satisfied in order that the action can be executed successfully. In other words, it ensures that the action is only executed in such data base states, where it is assured by the action semantics that only a valid, i.e. consistent, data base state will be produced by the execution. However, we have to make here an important restriction. The condition only *checks* the locally used part of the state. That is, it only guarantees consistency in this *local view* of the data base. During the action execution of other complex actions may be activated. Those actions by themselves are responsible for leaving their own local state consistent. It is easy to see that a consistent combination of in themselves consistent actions will produce a consistent combined state transformation. The action itself may be part of some larger unit which again will guarantee its (larger) local consistency. In this way, a hierarchy of consistent actions can be built, where each one guarantees consistency in its own environment and in combination total consistency will be assured.

The *escape clause* specified with an action name now can be explained. If a precondition is not satisfied, but also if the procedure part of the action cannot be executed, for example because some called action has a precondition which is not satisfied, the effect of the current action will be *nullified* (*backout* occurs) and the activity specified in the escape clause will be executed.

The operation in the escape clause may be any complex action or one of the two *built-in* actions:

abort	The surrounding activity is aborted in which the present action is contained.
cancel ("text")	The current action will not be executed but the calling activity will continue normally. The "text" specified will be returned to the calling routine via a specially provided parameter (e.g. Message in Fig. 10.11 b) to indicate the failure of the action.

a) Definition

```
operation insert employee escape cancel ('no insert')
    with time Insertion time;
    input external eno  of Emp-Number
                   fn   of First Name
                   ln   of Last Name
                   sal  of Salary
                   mno  of Machine Number
         data base m    is Machine (mno);
    output;
    precondition   not is-element Emp-Number eno and
                   not exists Employee (eno) and
                   is-element Machine m, cancel
    postcondition  is-element Emp-Number eno and
                   is-element Employee (eno) and
                   is-element Emp-Number (eno eno) and
                   is-element Name (fn ln) and
                   is-element Salary (sal eno) and
                   is-element Worker Machine (eno m);
    procedure
         sequence  insert Emp-Number eno
                   create Employee (eno)
                   insert Employee eno with Insertion time
                   insert First Name fn
                   insert Last Name ln
                   insert Salary sal
                   establish Name (fn ln)
                   establish Salary (sal eno)
                   establish Worker-Machine (eno m)
         endsequence
    end
```

b) Use

```
insert employee  (15308, 'John', 'Miller', 35000.00, M29) Message
```

Fig. 10.11 a, b. A complex action *insert employee*

The *postcondition* clause formalizes the local consistency condition that has to be satisfied by the result state of the action. In reality, this clause is redundant if we assume a correct precondition and a correct procedure part for the action, as this combination already ensures a consistent result state. The postcondition therefore can be used to statically *verify* the correctness of the action (as in program verification), or to dynamically *check* the result state to possibly detect errors in the action definition.

The *procedure clause* of a complex TH-model action may contain a set of *local action definitions.* These actions behave precisely like local procedures in a programming language, as for example PASCAL. The local actions are *not usable* outside of the containing procedure, i.e. they are not visible outside (cannot be exported), as would be the case in a full abstract data type language. Otherwise they have the format and can be used like any other complex action.

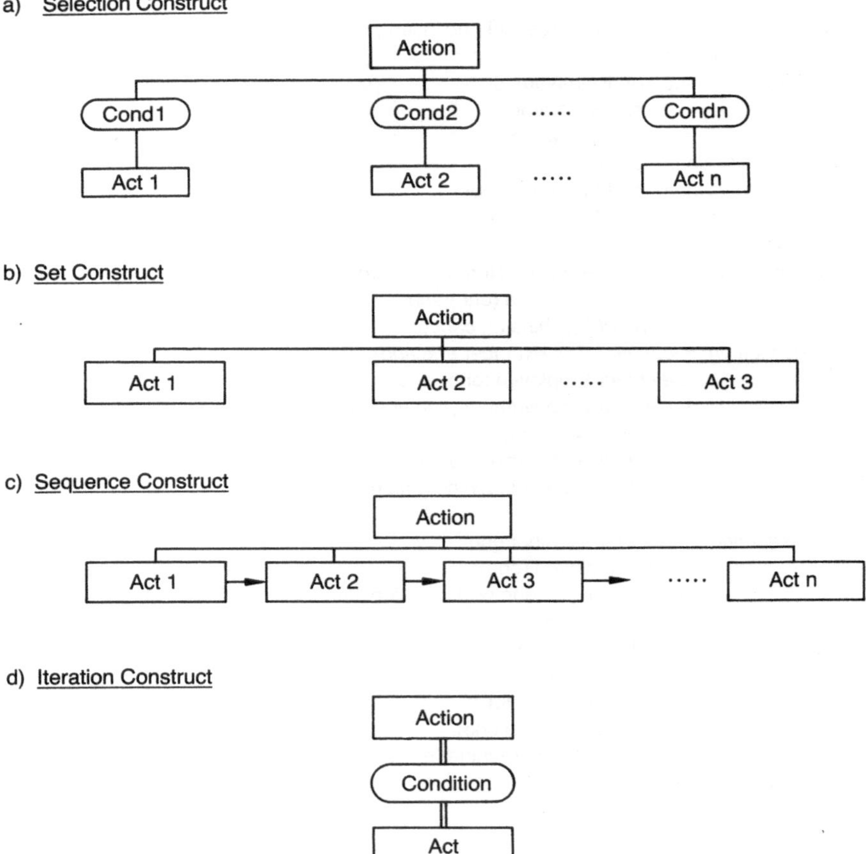

Fig. 10.12. The Action-operations of the TH-Model

The second part of the procedure is represented by the *procedure body*. In the TH-model the composition of the procedure body is restricted according to the application structuring principles introduced in [St1, St2]. For this part of the action definition, a graphic representation has been developed in THM (see [Ho]). It will be used in the following as it presents a clearer picture of the functional composition of actions than a purely textual definition. However, the other clauses of an action definition will only be represented partially in the graphs and additional textual specifications will have to be given to complete the definition.

In [St1, St2] four different operations are introduced to provide for the modularization of a functional description according to principles derived from structured programming.

Selection (Disjunction): One or more of a number of actions may be selected for execution with the help of some given condition (see Fig. 10.12a). If more than one of the conditions is satisfied the selected actions may be executed concurrently. In

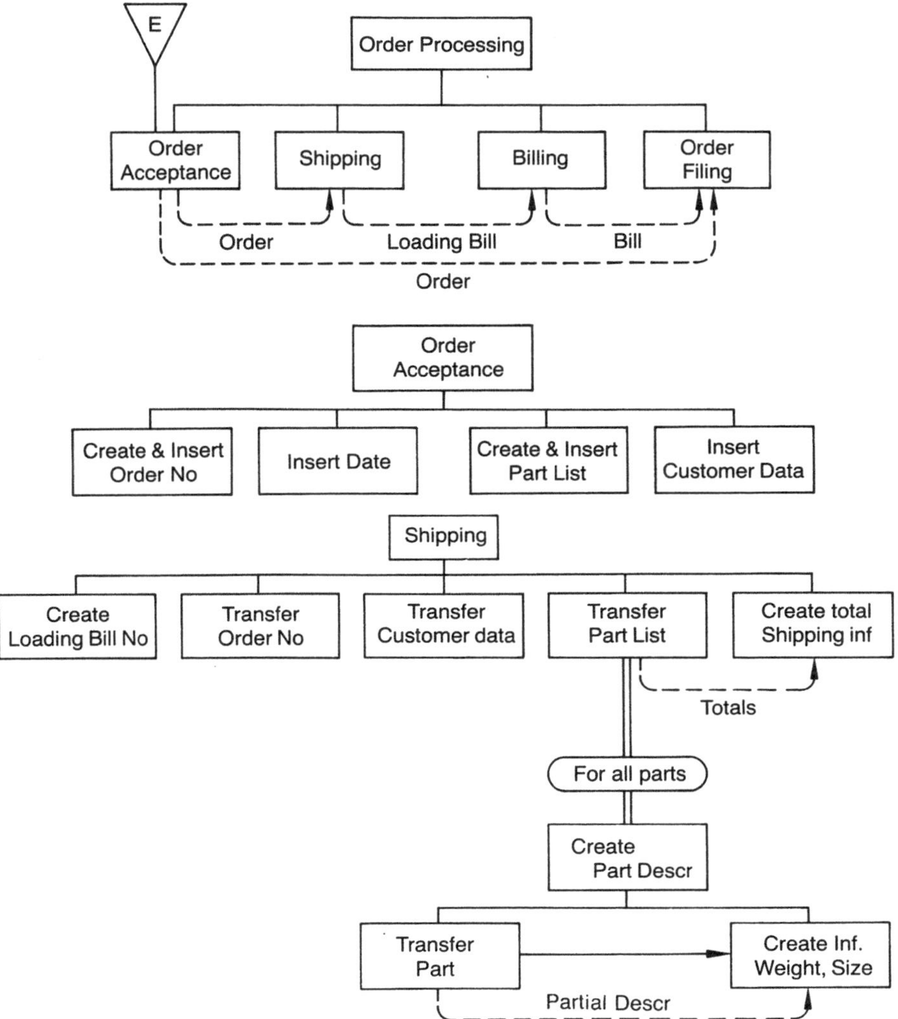

Fig. 10.13. *Order processing* as a THM Action Diagram

Fig. 10.12 a the diagram is to be read: The action "Action" consists of a selection operation selecting between the actions Act 1, Act 2, ..., Act n with the selection conditions Cond 1, Cond 2, ..., Cond n.

Set (Conjunction): All actions of the set will have to be executed in order to achieve the effect of the Group action (see Fig. 10.12b). The execution order is open, the actions may be executed concurrently.

Sequence: All actions of the construct have to be executed in the sequence indicated by the arrows in the graph (see Fig. 10.12c).

Iteration: The action Act will be executed repeatedly as long as the Condition has the value *true*. The test is performed *before* each execution of Act (see Fig. 10.12d).

With the help of these operations the procedure body of an action can easily be specified. Actually it can be used to graphically describe an application containing complex control flow between the contained actions. Fig. 10.13 specifies the complex action *order processing* as an action graph by using the principles explained above. In addition to the operational structure dashed lines are used to illustrate *input-output* behaviour of the contained actions. Such dependencies may give rise to the specification of execution sequences or at least to the specification of *start event* clauses to properly synchronize the action execution. The triangle construct with the letter E indicates that the whole complex action *order processing* is started by an external event E, e.g. some user action at a terminal.

This concludes our discussion of the Temporal Hierarchic Model and actually also our investigation of "less formal" semantic data base models.

The models presented in Chap. 8, 9 and 10 have been developed over a number of years, but all of them are still evolving. Many more models could be described, but with respect to the more formal orientation discussed in the first part of this book, the present selection seems sufficient. The most powerful of the models introduced here is THM. It actually has been developed to provide, together with additional components not discussed here, a full methodology for the development of data base and information system applications. Other such general techniques have been described in [OSV] and [OST] which are recommended for a reading.

11 Conclusion

The formalisms at the informations level and at the functions level of PART A can be classified as *definitional* (or axiomatic). Definitional specifications are logic theories, characterizing the universe of discourse implicitly in terms of its properties.

The formalism at the representation level of PART A, as well as all the formalisms of PART B are *constructive* (or operational). Constructive specifications use an abstract model (already a data model, in PART A, and the various semantic data models, in PART B), in the technical sense of a mathematical structure onto which the universe of discourse is mapped.

The techniques of PART A result in precise specifications, amenable to rigorous formal verification. The techniques of PART B, by staying close to natural language and by using graph diagrams extensively, cater to intuition and flexibility. By not insisting so much on mathematical rigor, they can cope with applications whose size, complexity and lack of precision (even apparent inconsistencies, in some cases) seem to defeat attempts to use the mathematically-oriented formalisms.

Figure 11.1 refers again to the semantic gap problem, mentioned in the General Introduction (Fig. 1.1), this time to summarize the paths followed in parts A and B, both of which converge ultimately to (conventional) data models and implementation on DBMSs adopting such data models.

Lines A and B can be integrated in at least two interesting ways:

- the representation level of PART A could lead first to a representation by a semantic (rather than by a conventional) data model;

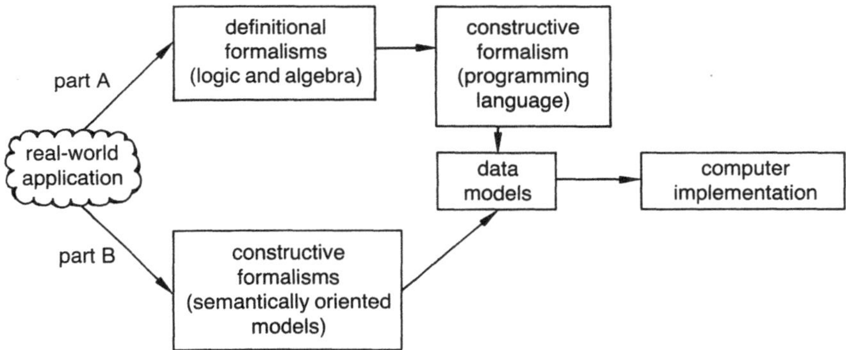

Fig. 11.1. The Formalisms used for Data Base Design

- the semantic data models of PART B could be, in turn, the object of formal specification, using grammatical and denotational techniques.

This integration, aiming to combine the advantages of precision with those of intuition and flexibility, together with the development of software tools incorporating and making easier to use the techniques discussed, are topics for continuing research.

12 References

Logical Formalism

Fundamentals

[En] H.B. Enderton – "A mathematical introduction to logic" – Academic Press (1972)

[Ha] D. Harel – "First-order dynamic logic" – Lecture Notes In Computer Science, vol. 68 – Springer-Verlag (1979)

[MP] Z. Manna and A. Pnueli – "Temporal verification of concurrent programs" – in "The correctness problem in computer science" – R. S. Boyer and J.S. Moore (eds.) – Academic Press (1981) 215–273

[RU] N. Rescher and A. Urquhart – "Temporal logic" – Springer-Verlag (1971)

Data Base Research

[BADW] A. Bolour, T.L. Anderson, L.J. Dekeyser and N.K.T. Wong – "The role of time in information processing – a survey" – ACM SIGMOD RECORD, 12, 3 (1982) 27–50

[CCF] J.M.V. de Castilho, M.A. Casanova and A.L. Furtado – "A temporal framework for data base specification" – Proc. of the 8th International Conference on Very Large Data Bases (1982) 280–291

[CF] M.A. Casanova and A.L. Furtado – "A family of temporal languages for the description of transition constraints" – in "Advances in Database Theory", vol. II – H. Gallaire, J. Minker and J.M. Nicolas (eds.) – Plenum Press (1984) 211–236

[GM] H. Gallaire and J. Minker (eds.) – "Logic and data bases" – Plenum Press (1978)

[GMN 1] H. Gallaire, J. Minker and J.M. Nicolas (eds.) – "Advances in data base theory" – Plenum Press (1980)

[GMN 2] H. Gallaire, J. Minker and J.M. Nicolas – "Logic and databases: an overview and survey" – Joint Report CGE/CERT/University of Maryland (1982)

[Ja] B.E. Jacobs – "On database logic" Journal of the ACM, 29, 2 (1982) 310–332

[Li] W. Lipski – "On databases with incomplete information" – Journal of the ACM, 28, 1 (1981) 41–70

[Ma] D. Maier – "The theory of relational databases" – Computer Science Press (1983)

[Se] A. Sernadas – "Temporal aspects of logical procedure definition" – Information Systems, 5 (1980) 167–187

Algebraic Formalism

Fundamentals

[GHM] J.V. Guttag, E. Horowitz, D.R. Musser – "The design of data type specifications" – in "Current trends in programming methodology" – R.T. Yeh (ed.) – Prentice-Hall (1978) 60–79

[GTW] J.A. Goguen, J.W. Thatcher and E.G. Wagner – "An initial algebra approach to the specification, correctness and implementation of abstract data types" – in "Current trends in programming methodology" – R.T. Yeh (ed.), vol. IV, Prentice-Hall (1978) 80–169

[Gu] J. Guttag – "Abstract data types and the development of data structures" – Communications of the ACM, 21, 12 (1978)

[Pa] C. Pair – "Sur les modeles des types abstraits algebriques" – Seminaire d'informatique theoretique – Universite de Paris VI et VII (1980)

Data Base Research

[BZ] M.L. Brodie and S.N. Zilles (eds.) – Proc. of the Workshop on Data Abstraction, Databases and Conceptual Modelling – SIGMOD Record, 11, 2 (1981)

[DMW] W. Dosch, G. Mascari and M. Wirsing – "On the algebraic specification of databases" – Proc. 8th International Conference on Very Large Data Bases (1982) 370–385

[EKW] H. Ehrig, H.J. Kreowski and H. Weber – "Algebraic specification schemes for data base systems" – Proc. 4th International Conference on Very Large Data Bases (1978) 427–440

[LMWW] P.C. Lockemann, H.C. Mayr, W. H. Weil and W.H. Wohlleber – "Data abstractions for data base systems" – ACM Transactions on Database Systems, 4, 1 (1979) 60–75

[VF] P.A.S. Veloso and A.L. Furtado – "Stepwise construction of algebraic specifications" – in "Advances in Database Theory", vol. II – H. Gallaire, J. Minker and J.M. Nicolas (eds.) – Plenum Press (1984) 321–352

Programming Language Formalism

Fundamentals

[Ea] J. Earley – "Toward an understanding of data structures" – Communications of the ACM, 14, 10 (1971) 617–627

[LZ] B.H. Liskov and S.N. Zilles – "Programming with abstract data types" – Proc. ACM Symposium on Very High Level Languages – SIGPLAN Notices 9, 4 (1974) 50–59

[LZ] B.H. Liskov and S.N. Zilles – "Programming with abstract data types" – SIGPLAN Notices 9, 4 (1974) 50–59

[Sch] J.T. Schwartz – "Principles of specification language design with some observations concerning the utility of specification languages" – in "Algorithm specification" – R. Rustin (ed.) – Prentice-Hall (1972)

[We 1] P. Wegner – "The Vienna Definition Language" – ACM Computing Surveys, 4, 1 (1972) 5–63

Data Base Research

[CB] M.A. Casanova and P.A. Bernstein – "A formal system for reasoning about programs accessing a relational database" – ACM Transactions on Programming Languages and Systems, 2, 3 (1980) 386–414

[MBW] J. Mylopoulos, P.A. Bernstein and H.K.T. Wong – "A language facility for designing database-intensive applications" – ACM Transactions on Database System, 5, 2 (1980) 185–217

[Ro] N. Roussopoulos – "CSDL: a conceptual schema definition language for the design of data base applications" – IEEE Transactions on Software Engineering, 5, 5 (1979) 481–496

[SW] A.M. Schettini and J. Winkowski – "Towards a programming language for manipulating relational data bases" – in "Formal description of programming concepts II" – D. Bjorner (ed.) – North-Holland (1983) 265–280

Generative Formalism

Fundamentals

[CER] V. Claus, H. Ehrig and G. Rozenberg (eds.) – "Graph grammars and their application to computer science and biology" – Springer-Verlag (1979)

[ENR] H. Ehrig, M. Nagl and G. Rozenberg (eds.) – "Graph-grammars and their application to computer science" – Springer-Verlag (1983)
[He] W. Hesse – "A correspondence between W-grammars and formal systems of logic and its application to formal language description" – Technical Report TUM-INFO-7727 – Technische Universität München (1977)
[Pe] J.E.L. Peck – "Two-level grammars in action" – Proc. 6th IFIP World Computer Congress (1974) 317–321

Data Base Research

[EK] H. Ehrig and H.J. Kreowski – "Applications of graph grammar theory to consistency, synchronization and scheduling in database systems" – Information Systems, 5 (1980) 225–238
[FVC] A.L. Furtado, P.A.S. Veloso and M.A. Casanova – "A grammatical approach to data bases" – Proc. 9th IFIP World Computer Congress (1983) 705–710
[Ki] C.M.R. Kintala – "Attributed grammars for query language translations" – Proc. 2nd ACM SIGACT-SIGMOD Symposium on Principles of Database Systems (1983) 137–148
[LMP] H. Laine, O. Maanavilja and E. Peltola – "Grammatical data base model" – Information Systems, 4, 4 (1979) 257–267.
[RB] D. Ridjanovic and M.L. Brodie – "Defining database dynamics with attribute grammars" – Information Processing Letters, 14, 3 (1982) 132–138.

Denotational Formalism

Fundamentals

[BJ] D. Bjorner and C.B. Jones – "Formal specification and software development" – Prentice-Hall (1982)
[Sco] D. Scott – "Logic and programming languages" – Communications of the ACM, 20, 9 (1977) 634–641
[Te] R.D. Tennent – "The denotational semantics of programming languages" – Communications of the ACM, 19, 8 (1976) 437–453

Data Base Research

[BL] D. Bjorner and H.H. Lovengreen – "Formalization of database systems and a formal definition of IMS" – Proc. 8th International Conference on Very Large Data Bases (1982) 334–347
[LP] G. Louis and A. Pirotte – "A denotational definition of the semantics of DRC, a Domain Relational Calculus" – Proc. 8th International Conference on Very Large Data Bases (1982) 348–356
[LS] W. Lammersdorf and J.W. Schmidt – "Semantic definition of Pascal/R" – reports 73–74, Univ. of Hamburg (1980)
[NO] E.J. Neuhold and T. Olnhoff – "The Vienna Development Method (VDM) and its use for the specification of a relational data base system" – Proc. 8th IFIP World Computer Congress (1980) 3–16

Complementarity

Fundamentals

[Do] J.E. Donahue – "Complementary definitions of programming language semantics" – Springer-Verlag (1976)

[HL] C.A.R. Hoare and P.E. Lauer – "Consistent and complementary formal theories of the semantics of programming languages" – Acta Informatica, 3 (1974) 135–153
[Pa] F.G. Pagan – "Formal specification of programming languages" – Prentice-Hall (1981)
[We2] P. Wegner – "Programming language semantics" – in "Formal semantics of programming languages" – R. Rustin(ed) – Prentice-Hall (1972) 149–248

Data Base Research

[VCF] P.A.S. Veloso, J.M.V. de Castilho and A.L. Furtado – "Systematic derivation of complementary specifications" – Proc. 7th International Conference on Very Large Data Bases (1981) 409–421
[CVF] M.A. Casanova, P.A.S. Veloso and A.L. Furtado – "Formal data base specification – an eclectic perspective" – Proc. of the 3rd ACM SIGACT/SIGMOD Symposium on Principles of Database Systems (1984) 110–118

Semantic Data Models

[Ab] R. Abrial – "Data semantics" – in "Data base management" – J.W. Klimbie and K.L. Koffeman (eds.) – North Holland (1974) 1–60
[Bi] H. Biller – "Die Semantik von Datenbanken" – Dissertation – Inst. Informatik, Univ. Stuttgart (1976)
[BN1] H. Biller and E.J. Neuhold – "Concepts for the conceptual schema" – in "Architecture and models in data base management systems" – G.M. Nijssen (ed.) – North Holland (1977) 1–30
[BN2] H. Biller and E.J. Neuhold – "Semantics of data bases: the semantics of data models" – Information Systems, 3, 1 (1978) 11–30
[Che1] P.P. Chen – "The entity-relationship model: towards a unified view of data" – Transactions on Database Systems, 1, 11 (1976) 77–84
[Che2] P.P. Chen (ed.) – "Entity-relationship approach to system analysis and design" – North-Holland (1980)
[Che3] P.P. Chen (ed.) – "Entity-relationship approach to information modelling and analysis" – ER-Institute (1981)
[Co] E.F. Codd – "Extending the database relational model to capture more meaning" – Transactions on Database Systems, 4, 4 (1979) 397–434
[Da] C.J. Date – "An introduction to database systems" – 2 vols. – Addison-Wesley (1983)
[DJNY] C.G. Davis, S. Jajodia, A.P. Ng and R.T. Yeh – "Entity-relationship approach to software engineering" – North-Holland (1983)
[Fl] J.J. Florentin – "Consistency auditing in data bases" – Computer Journal, 17, 1 (1974) 52–58
[Ho] A. Horndasch – "Entwurf und Anwendung von Datenbankenoperationen" – Report 9/82 – Inst. Informatik, Univ. Stuttgart (1982)
[HS] A. Horndasch and U. Schiel – "THM/CSL: A language for conceptual schema specification" – Report 5/83 – Inst. Informatik, Univ. Stuttgart (1983).
[ISO] ISO TC97/SC5/WG3 – "Concepts and terminology for the conceptual schema and information base" – J.J. von Griethuysen (ed.) (1982)
[OST] T.W. Olle, H.G. Sol and C.J. Tully (eds.) – "Information system design methodologies" – North-Holland (1983)
[OSV] T.W. Olle, H.G. Sol and A.A. Verrijn-Stuart (eds.) – Information systems design: a comparative review" – North-Holland (1982)
[RM] N. Roussopoulos and J. Mylopoulos – "Using semantic networks for data base management" – Proc. of the 1st Conference on Very Large Data Bases (1975) 144–172
[Sa] C.S. dos Santos – "Caracterizacao sistematica de restricoes de integridade em bancos de dados" – PhD thesis – Pontificia Universidade Catolica do Rio de Janeiro (1980)
[Sc1] U. Schiel – "The temporal hierarchic data model (THM)" – Report 10/82 – Inst. Informatik, Univ Stuttgart (1982)
[Sc2] U. Schiel – "A semantic data model and its mapping to the internal relational model" – in "Data bases – roles and structures" – P. Stocker, M. Atkinson and P. Grey (eds.) – Cambridge University Press (1983)

[Sc 3] U. Schiel – "An abstract introduction to the temporal-hierarchic data model (THM)" – Proc. of the 9th Conference on Very Large Data Bases" (1983) 322–330

[SFNC] U. Schiel, A.L. Furtado, E.J. Neuhold and M.A. Casanova – "Towards multi-level and modular conceptual schemas" – Information Systems, 9, 1 (1984) 43–57

[SNF] C.S. dos Santos, E.J. Neuhold and A.L. Furtado – "A data type approach to the entity-relationship model" – in "Entity-relationship approach to systems analysis and design" – P.P. Chen (ed.) – North-Holland (1980)

[SS] J.M. Smith and D.C.P. Smith – "Data base abstractions: aggregation and generalization" – Transactions on Data Base Systems, 2, 2 (1977) 105–133

[St 1] R. Studer – "Functional specification of a decision support system" – Proc. of the 6th Conference on Very Large Data Bases (1979) 85–93

[St 2] R. Studer – "A dialog interface for data base applications" – Proc. of the 7th Conference on Very Large Data Bases (1980) 167–182

[Su] B. Sundgren – "An infological approach to data bases" – Report 7 – Statistika Centralbyran, Stockholm (1973)

[TF] T.J. Teorey and J.P. Fry – "Design of database structures" – Prentice-Hall (1982)

[TL] D.C. Tsichritzis and F.H. Lochovsky – "Data models" – Prentice-Hall (1982)

[Wa] I. Walter – "View modelling based on the semantic data model THM" – Univ. Stuttgart (1983)

13 Subject Index

abstract data type 94
- model 54
- state 54
- structure 12
- universe of discourse 54
abstraction 54
active system 11
aggregation 78
algebraic formalism 19
application oriented approach 3
assert fact 10
attribute 72
attribute-value pair 72
axiom 13
axiomatic theory 15

basic action 95
- type 60

characteristic 62
characterization 79
class 87
- relation 87
clock 90
complex state manipulation action 99
conceptual design framework 7
conceptual view 52
conditional equation 13
consistency constraint 65
construction rule 95
conventional data base 57
current time 90

data base application 1
- - interpretation 56
- - management system (DBMS) 1
- - schema 57
- definition language 57, 77
- manipulation language 93
- model 1
- structure 14
declare constraint 12
deny fact 10
derived relationship 83
- type 62

deterministic program 30
domain 65
dynamic consistency condition 58

elementary sentence 53
encapsulation 13
entity 54, 72, 87
- instance 67
- key 75
- primary key 75
- relation 75
- set 72
entity-relationship diagram 75
- model 48, 71
escape clause 100
event 11
existence constraint 83
- dependency 62

first-order logic 13
first-order language 15
functions level 8

generalization 78
grouping 78

history class 90
- environment 91
hypernotion 31
hyperrule 33

identification constraint 83
identifying set 63
implicit constraint 12
indexing type 82
information level 8
inherent relationship 83
inheritance 79
integrity constraint 7
interpretation 23

logic formalism 13
logical data base model 47

logical data definition language 56
– – language 56, 67
– schema 57
– state description 56

manipulation longuage 77
member relation 87
metaproduction 31
metarule 32
modal operator 16
model 54
modularization 9

natural language interpretation 53
nucleus type 60

object 52
observability condition 20
observation 20
operation 30
operational facility 93

parallel execution 11
parameter passing 99
postcondition 101
pre-condition 10, 100
predicate 31
– calculus 15
– symbol 13
procedural constraint 12
procedure 14
production rule 14
property 52
– instance 67

query operation 3

reachable state 27
real world state 52
reality 52
refinement 8, 23
relation 54, 87
– declaration 65
– instance 67
– name 29
relational model 12
– program variable 29
– term 29
relationship 52, 72
– primary key 76
– relation 75
representation language 53
– level 8

semantic data model 47
– domain 35
– equation 36
– framework 51
– function 36
serial execution 11
side effect 21
sort 19
sort-of-interest 19
standard interpretation 54
start event 99
state 9
– description 53
statement 30
static constraint 9
sufficient completeness 20
syntactic domain 35

table 75
temporal extension 16
– hierarchic model 87
time 90
transition 9
tuple 81
type 54
– declaration 59
– definition 60

universe 16
– of discourse 52
update function 3

valid state 9, 26
value 72
– set 72
verification 41

w-grammar 30